HAYWIRE

Luljeta Lleshanaku was born in Elbasan, Albania in 1968. Under Enver Hoxha's Stalinist dictatorship, she grew up under house arrest. Lleshanaku was not permitted to attend college or publish her poetry until the weakening and eventual collapse of the regime in the early 1990s. She later studied Albanian philology at the University of Tirana, and has worked as a schoolteacher, literary magazine editor and journalist. She won the prestigious International Kristal Vilenica Prize in 2009, and has had a teaching post at the University of Iowa and a fellowship from the Black Mountain Institute at the University of Nevada, Las Vegas. She has given readings in America, Europe and in Ireland at the Poetry Now Festival in Dún Laoghaire in 2010.

Haywire: New & Selected Poems (Bloodaxe Books, 2011) is her first British publication, and includes work from two editions published in the US by New Directions, *Fresco: Selected Poems* (2002), which drew on four collections published in Albania from 1992 to 1999, and *Child of Nature* (2010), a book of translations of later poems, as well as a number of new, previously untranslated poems. Launched at Aldeburgh Poetry Festival in November 2011, *Haywire* is a Poetry Book Society Recommended Translation.

LULJETA LLESHANAKU

HAYWIRE

NEW & SELECTED POEMS

BLOODAXE BOOKS

ISBN: 978 1 85224 913 7

This edition first published 2011 by
Bloodaxe Books Ltd,
Highgreen,
Tarset,
Northumberland NE48 1RP.

www.bloodaxebooks.com
For further information about Bloodaxe titles
please visit our website or write to
the above address for a catalogue.

Supported by
ARTS COUNCIL
ENGLAND

Cover design: Neil Astley & Pamela Robertson-Pearce.

Printed in Great Britain by
Bell & Bain Limited, Glasgow, Scotland.

CONTENTS

TRANSLATORS
AG Ani Gijka
AJ Albana Lleshanaku
AK Alban Kupi
DW Daniel Weissbort
HI Henry Israeli
JG Joanna Goodman
NC Noci Deda
LL Luljeta Lleshanaku
LQ Lluka Qafoku
QS Qazim Sheme
SQ Shpresa Qatipi
UB Ukzenel Buçpapa

INTRODUCTION

Luljeta Lleshanaku is a pioneer of Albanian poetry. She speaks with a completely original voice, her imagery and language always unexpected and innovative. Her poetry has little connection to poetic styles past or present in America, Europe, or the rest of the world. And, interestingly enough, it is not connected to anything in Albanian poetry either. We have in Lleshanaku a completely original poet.

The fact that she is writing in Albania today is significant. There was an upsurge in Albanian literature following the collapse in 1990 of the harsh Stalinist dictatorship. Poets and novelists who had grown up in a totalitarian society that was in many ways more oppressive than the darkest years of Stalin's reign in the Soviet Union were given almost overnight the freedom to write. Established poets like Fates Arapi wrote new and candid verse, while the younger poets were energetic but rudderless after having been nurtured on Socialist Realism. All this poetry that came out of the hope, fear, hunger, and despair of Albania's desperate post-Stalinist 1990s is wild and creative, reflecting the chaotic but hopeful situation in Albania. Albanian literary critics eyed this development with a mix of fear and ecstasy. Unruly though the new writing might at times have appeared, what was apparent was that it was very original, because the poets had had virtually no contacts with the literature of the outside world. Lleshanaku's voice is the clearest to come out of this melting pot.

The unusualness of contemporary Albanian writing is linked to the unusual course of Albanian literature, which has the curious distinction of having both a long and ancient tradition, but also being very new. At the turn of the 20th century, Albanian was the last of the European languages without an official writing system. (Turkish was the official language.) Writers who chose to write in the spoken Albanian idiom used Arabic, Greek, or Latin script, depending on their education. The bulk of modern Albanian poetry was still oral and epic, sung by bards – 'A living laboratory for the study of ancient times,' according to Ismail Kadare, Albania's foremost writer. The dichotomy between an ancient oral and a new written literature stems from Albania's turbulent history. While

9

the rest of Europe was experiencing the Renaissance and the Enlightenment, Albania was under Ottoman rule, which viewed the Albanian language as a dangerous nationalistic weapon and forbade it to be taught in schools or used in any official capacity. And while Europe was in the midst of the literary ferment of the early 20th century, Albania was still trying to establish an alphabet and making the first attempts at a national literature. Gjergj Fishta, a national folk poet, finally proposed a standardised Latin orthography, which was adopted in 1909.

Luljeta Lleshanaku was born in 1968, during a crucial turning point in Albanian history. The People's Socialist Republic of Albania was celebrating the 22nd anniversary of its Stalinist regime. Seven years earlier Albania's dictator, Enver Hoxha, had isolated himself from his last ally, the Soviet Union, outraged at Nikita Krushchev's denunciation of Stalin, and shifted his allegiance to China's Chairman Mao.

When Mao launched his devastating Cultural Revolution in 1966, Enver Hoxha vied to outdo him. And he did. A great anti '-isms' campaign was launched in Albania to cleanse literature of all non-Marxist elements and 'alien ideological manifestations'. Poetry and prose were no longer to be tainted by: abstract humanism, anarchism, bourgeois objectivism, bureaucratism, conservatism, decadentism, ethnologism, folklorism, formalism, imperialism, individualism, intellectualism, mysticism, nihilism, patriarchalism, revisionism, or sentimentalism, to name a few. Many foreign hooks were banned, among them the Old Testament, the New Testament, the Koran, the Talmud, and all Buddhist texts. Albania was declared the first atheist nation of the world, and churches and mosques were torn down or converted into warehouses or local "culture" centers. Ancient icons and religious monuments were destroyed, precious books and manuscripts were burned.

Poets and novelists were forced to volunteer to strengthen their ties to the land by working in the fields. A piece of writing that manifested the slightest deviation, or perceived deviation, from the new official policy could land a writer in prison, a labour camp, or worse. As many poets were to find out, even the most unequivocal Communist stance in a poem was subject to being interpreted as anti-Communist propaganda. Visar Zhiti, for instance, a 22-year-old rising star on the Albanian literary scene of the early 1970s, was persecuted and finally imprisoned for ten years after sending his poetry manuscript to Nairn Frasheri Publishers. The verse that triggered his downfall:

No, no,
No bootblack will ever shine my shoes!
I do not want people at my feet.

To the untrained eye these lines might represent a youthful call for equality. The censor, however, interpreted them as an outright expression of capitalist-bourgeois contempt for the toiling bootblack.

And yet one of the unexpected results of the Albanian Cultural Revolution was that many prose writers turned to poetry, since it proved easier to follow the strict guidelines of Socialist Realism in the more concise forms of verse. While Lleshanaku was growing up, poetry was everywhere: in books, magazines, leaflets, on the radio. There were many public readings. The first poems she would have encountered would have followed Party dogma closely. Much of that poetry is difficult to read today with its rambling proclamations of party ideology. Some major Albanian poets of the 1960s and 1970s, such as Dritero Agolli, managed to express their Communist conviction in strong language, without a trace of irony:

I would have crawled through the mud,
Crushed and pulverised, crippled forever,
My arms slashed off at the elbow,
Rather than utter, 'Long Live King Zog!'
But I sing Enver Hoxha's praises.

And in another poem Agolli writes:

I carried the earth of your fields
In a woollen sack
Under my coat
To bring it
To the Writers' League.

Other poets, such as Ismail Kadare, chose themes that endeavoured to steer clear of anything that might possibly be seen as ideologically questionable. As had been the case with writers during the darkest years of Stalinism in the Soviet Union, successful Albanian poets and novelists became master jugglers of nuance and evasiveness, which at times led to powerful works despite the impossible stric-

11

tures. Much of Kadare's poetry (and prose) centred on the distant past, with Homeric or Ottoman themes:

> To me you were as impregnable as Troy,
> A Troy I could never conquer.
> To me you were indecipherable,
> More indecipherable than the Etruscan inscriptions.
>
> Only in my dreams, ah, in my dreams
> Have I grasped your thick hair.
> I felt more delight in conquering you
> Than all the Greeks felt at the fall of Troy.
>
> Only in my dreams are you decipherable,
> You, my sweet Etruscan girl.

In a country where reading was one of the only pleasures still allowed, the poets who managed to publish were guaranteed a wide readership, as miners, longshoremen, and factory workers lined up to buy their newest books. The People's Socialist Republic of Albania, with a population of three million, was a nation of poetry bestsellers.

Though Luljeta Lleshanaku was born at the height of Albania's Cultural Revolution, she was raised during the even darker years that followed. In 1972 Richard Nixon travelled to Beijing, and Enver Hoxha, outraged at what he saw as Chairman Mao's betrayal of Communism, began distancing himself from China. A decade and a half of Albania's total isolation from the outside world and increasing oppression followed. There was an almost complete moratorium on the circulation of foreign books, and translations of foreign literature practically ground to a halt. In his recent essay 'The Dictator's Library', Bashkim Shehu, one of Albania's foremost young novelists, took a walk through what used to be the restricted 'R' section of the National Library in Tirana – the only place in Albania (besides the Dictator's luxury villa) where one could find a French copy of Agatha Christie, Baudelaire, or the Dictator's favourite contemporary French poet, Edouard Glissant.

> Aragon and Rafael Alberti had been accused of betraying Communism, like Sartre, who was even accused of being a key representative of French imperialism. I found many books by Sartre, even an Esperanto translation of *L'existentialisme est un humanisme*, and another on microfilm. Why have the

National Library order an Esperanto translation of a book, and a microfilm, only to stamp a restrictive 'R' on them? Also restricted was a bibliography of the works of Cervantes – which, I admit, was totally beyond my comprehension. And then came a whole series of R's covering the whole philosophy section, from Plato's works and Aristotle's *De memoria et reminiscentia*, all the way through to modern works, among them a Cuban edition of Hegel's *The Phenomenology of the Spirit*. Even the philosophy books of György Lukacs, the staunchest Marxist critic of the 20th century, were restricted. The whole of philosophy was saddled with R's, except for Marx, Engels, Lenin, and Stalin.

The major poets who had established themselves in the 50s and 60s tackled the new state of affairs in different ways. Dritëro Agolli, who became the president of the Albanian Writers Union in 1973, was perhaps the most successful poet of the 1970s. (His 1974 long narrative poem *Mother Albania* sold over a hundred thousand copies.) His work became increasingly ideological, though he was not above turning to his readers in a stage-aside:

Forgive me for being a bore,
For filling my poems with didactics,
With workaday agitprop.

Mark Gurakutii and Luan Qafezezi, a generation older than Agolli (they were both born in 1922), wrote almost exclusively political poems that are practically unreadable outside the parameters of Stalinist Albania. Other poets, such as Dhori Qiriazi, published less hut tried to balance propaganda with non-political poems. Many other poets simply fell silent.

Luljeta Lleshanaku was 17 when Enver Hoxha died in 1985. During the next five years the People's Socialist Republic of Albania, still a Stalinist state under its new dictator, Ramiz Alia, began to disintegrate. After over a decade of absolute isolation from the world, with most of its national budget poured into armaments, Albania had run itself into the ground.

The dictatorship finally came to an end in December 1990. The first years of liberty were perhaps even more frightening and chaotic, as Albania's infrastructure continued to crumble, one government after the other collapsing, but for the first time in the country's history there was complete freedom of expression.

13

Lleshanaku quickly established herself as a powerful poetic voice, but one totally contrary to that of her generation. Her contemporaries, who had come of age with the decline and collapse of the Stalinist state, wrote verse loudly voicing the terror that had been and the terror that was perhaps to come. There was a strong literary reaction against all the norms and precepts of Socialist Realism, and yet political and social themes continued to be the principal driving force behind most of Albanian poetry of the late 1980s and early 1990s. Poets who had been raised in a literary world of Socialist Realism were ready to react against it and attack it, but had difficulty breaking free from its schooling. To quote one of Albania's foremost poets, Koce Petriti:

My soles were ripped, I patched them up.
I know what stone lies in my path.
I tread on it and write on it
my own humanitarian verse.

But one of the elements that distinguishes Luljeta Lleshanaku's poetry is the absence of direct social and political commentary. Her poetry's remarkable variety of themes, which avoids simplistic reactions to a terrible past and an unstable present and future, is perhaps one of the elements that makes her poems contemporary classics of world literature. The imagery and rhythms captured in the masterful translations gathered under these covers make her poems as compelling in English as they are in Albanian. She speaks individually to her readers, the mark of a true poet able to transcend time and culture.

PETER CONSTANTINE
Introduction to *Fresco* (2002)

FRESCO

I

Memory

There is no prophecy, only memory.
What happens tomorrow
has happened a thousand years ago
the same way, to the same end –
and does my ancient memory
say that your false memory
is the history of the featherhearted bird
transformed into a crow atop a marble mountain?
The same woman will be there
on the path to reincarnation
her cage of black hair
her generous and bitter heart
like an amphora full of serpents.

There is no prophecy, things happen
as they have before –
death finds you in the same bed
lonely and without sorrow, shadowless
as trees wet with night.

There is no destiny, only laws of biology;
fish splash in water
pine trees breathe on mountains.

Birds and Carbon

The time arrives
when wiping traces of carbon off with their sleeves
poets return to the season of birds.

We recognise birds by their poses
the fleeting arcs of flight
the same arcs tour guides make with pointers
when stopping along the streets of
Waterloo, Ithaca, Cairo, Berlin....

That's where history, mine and everyone's,
rests for a moment to take a deep breath.
Time stands still
the rest of life but smoke, luggage lifted and set down,
a conductor's small flag waving in our imaginations.

I can't remember the last time I held my breath –
was it summer? August? The sky scratched
with fresh red lines
like a gardener's palm. A pair of birds
joyfully encircled my home.
I exhaled, and a lone tree quivering in a field
transformed them into two pieces of paper
condemned to forever
somersault in the wind.

Peninsula

My shadow stretches over the street
peninsula of fear
with coordinates that shake in the wind
like last week's wet blankets
hung out to dry.

The frightened child or the nervous woman
(the last brushstroke is missing)
the trembling border that separates them
the zigzag of smoke
from a forgotten cigarette.

At first I had only one eye
big and blue and dilated...
Now I have two
and a strip of sand between them
that dries and thickens
from day to day.

And a wind constantly shifting directions
pursuing clues left by the fossils
of extinct fish.

Neurosis

relentlessly pursues its daily ration
like a cat circling the cracked
        plate of my patience,
scrounging for what it can find.

It slinks between the feet
of those gathered around the table
the glare of a television screen
from across the room
floating like a glacier
through our frozen imaginations.

Mother's voice rustles, wrinkling the silence.
'Winter is nearing... we have to fix the door...'

Her daughter burns blue as an alcohol flame
and the molecules of air that surround her
reproduce, splitting and multiplying
impregnating themselves
drowning with desire for the distant seas.

The Woman and the Scissors

I remember the scissors
that cut thick strips of newspaper
to seal cracks on stove pipes
and the scissors that trimmed my soft nails
delicate as pleurae

and later on
my sister's small scissors that cut
the silk thread of her embroidery, blue loops
wound tightly round two fingers of her right hand
while I watched a man shoveling snow
and heard rocks struck
and saw an acacia tree
branches covered in ice
swaying majestically, conspicuously,
like a nine-year-old on a swing,
with green bangs
and white stockings.

And then came my escape from the anxiety of scissors
an all-consuming appetite for books
the betrayal of my parents' simple dream:
a tailor's large scissors
tracing white chalk lines.

The Woman and the Giraffes

The woman remembers:
once she was a member
of a family of giraffes
their skin so warm
it baked the air to terracotta.
A giraffe's strength resides in its neck
in its long and muscled neck.
Its suffering, too, resides in the neck
in its bending over tropical trees.

One day, the entire herd was blotted out.
Their heads, slender knees, spotted backs, gone.
Only necks remained, oblique giraffe necks
confounded amidst blank paper
like boarding ladders on an airport runway
clumsily dragging themselves along
after the planes take off.

Winter

Winter approaches
the bothersome sound of flies and cicadas dwindling.
Light fades over the poker game
the moon transplanted into the sky
like a healthy kidney into a weak body.
The pain lifts
but we remain lost, confused,
cloaked in condensation
like a busy downtown phone booth.

Venetian blinds slide shut
slicing off fingers of streetlight.
Tattered, dark squares alternate
where birds cross in migration,
a wall from which paintings are being removed.
An unconscious man's dream in black and white
is stopped short by a nurse's cough.
My body pressed against your ribs through the long night
like the earth by its latitudes, my last geographical memories
lying in frayed maps deep inside the city archives.

In the morning, mother stands in the same place
preparing coffee
plump, clean, healthy as an Easter egg.
Afraid of decalcification, the inevitable,
afraid of shattering.

Chamomile Breath

We never talk about death, mother
like married people who never speak of sex
doctors who never mention blood
the postman who no longer realises he is holding his breath.

But fear of it graces everything you touch
the way a cotton field quivers
as a man strides through it.

In the morning
your chamomile breath
rises over the wrinkled pillow
adorned with white ubiquitous strands of hair
and black metal clips.

Don't wait for death to come noisily, mother,
dressed in wild, coloured cloth
bells on its elbows and knees
like the Man of Carnivals
or a morris dancer at the end of May.

You will see instead a child with spindly legs
and a thick crop of hair
a child who never had the chance to grow up.
Haven't you ever heard the saying:
death is so close to birth
they are like nostrils on a face
on the verge of a sneeze.

And the Sun Is Extinguished

And the sun is extinguished
like the little red light that disappears
when the elevator stops.

I can't remember which is our floor –
the third, fifth, or the hundred and first...
but it always ends the same way:
a slap of cold air
the look of impatience
on the faces of those
waiting to get on.

Perhaps My Mother

She remembers her wedding
and the levy that followed –
three children with patched knees
little sharks
shadowing the white wreath of a ship.

She remembers the black violin
on the shelf
the depressions in its body
and on her husband's shirts
the impression of scaffolding,
concrete. She remembers
the petroleum pipeline, her harsh voice
dirty pockets, the hairs over her lip.
She remembers the neighbours' tiled rooftops sloping
into her small courtyard and the riverwind
scavenging, swallowing back days.

She remembers the cold, bruised
hands of midwives
inside her
fire irons poking coal
into flame.

She remembers the sick baby
her frantic fingers
on the morgue window
a dead soldier's
protruding feet.

I've never met this woman.
I only know the details
and a sweet old woman frightened out of superfluous sleep.
Perhaps my mother
an apple tree and cypress grafted together
a flickering neon light.

Nocturne. Soft Whistle

Now I imagine you, mother,
as you nap, snoring, one breast
sunk like a moon into sweet waters.
Are you frightened by thoughts of the insulin
the doctor prescribed this morning?
My little, old mother
past tense
or future past
wrapped inside the grey shawl
of an acrylic poem.

Sleep is short
there is hardly time
to dream about what life once held for you:
one white child, one black child
chasing a ball of yarn along the rug.

I know the way you startle awake.
I know the shattered door
at the entrance to your glass house.

But don't let me disturb your nap
with the swirling of my imagination,
a flock of zinc birds flying low to the ground.
Even in my dreams I cannot quell
the waves slapping against the hull
of a boat that follows the current.

The Night Will Soon Be Over...

When night arrives
trees strip off their shadows...

and
quarrel in the warm lake.

The moon's white calves
flash through the rushes.

The owl's eye
like a drop of mercury
slides across the nude body of the world.

A few more hours
and the night will be over...

remaining only in the pleats of a black cloak
slung over the branches of a cypress tree.

More Than a Retrospective

I was born of a dead hope
like a sprig of grass
between sidewalk slabs.

I learned my first words
behind an ill-fitted door.

I came to understand
the properties of light and darkness
through the cracks in my body
a clay body not wholly fired.

I learned to sing
the way a cold draft learns to navigate
between two clumsy lovers.

But like a whore's dirty underpants
I am not growing used to sadness...

One dead hope
catches up to the next
like one bus approaching another
then the stop.

Clear Hours

During clear hours
I am like the lonely hunchbacked tree
        on the slope of a hill.
Beneath my shade
rest weary travellers.

I count the rings around my trunk
I count the knots and navels
I scratch beneath my cracked bark –
a woman's nightmare.

I count white days, warm days
I count the rotations of the sun rolling
into darkness, I count nights of moonlight
nights of lightning
when I embrace you from behind, when I pull away from you
as streams of water from a shower tile.

I count yellow days
and tighten my grip on the test tube of all days.
Many are the friends who disappear
few who return.
        My black blood circulates, my black memory
turns back on itself
and drowns
in the primeval silence of creation.

Sunday Bells

My soul
beats like a tongue
against the side of a bell.

Listen.
It's the Sunday bells
the Sunday bells of high mass
when the priest preaches forgiveness
and we all lay flowers on graves.

What Is Known

The search for unknown words
is a complete failure.
They have all been discovered.
They are round and soft, without mystery
little planets festering with ants too tired
to mount a tramp's shoe.

Rosary in hand
the words count crimson drops
of silence dripping from above
and repeat themselves over and over
like demented men.

But they take pride in their age.
After all, they are exhibits in a museum
and I, transitory, passing before them
can only cloud their glass
with my breath.

II

Fresco

Now there is no gravity. Freedom is meaningless.
I weigh no more than a hair
on a starched collar.
Lips meet in the ellipsis at the end of a drowning
confession; on the sand, a crab closes its claws hermetically
and moves one step forward and two steps to the right.
It was long ago when I first broke into a shudder
at the touch of your fingers;
no more shyness, no more healing, no more death.
Now I am light as an Indian feather, and can easily reach the moon
a moon clean as an angel's sex
on the frescoes of the church.
Sometimes I can even see asteroids dying like drones
in ecstasy for their love, their queen.

Electrolytes

For a long time now
your kisses have burned me
and your clean body frightened me
like sheets in a surgery ward
and your breath disappearing in my lungs
is like lilies dropped into a cesspool
in the dead of winter.

For a long time now
I have felt ashamed of my freedom.
Every day I pull a stake off your fence
and burn it for warmth.

My freedom... your freedom...
An atmosphere alive with electricity
my soul pawned for a nickel
yours slowly deserted by its ions
and growing smaller every day.

Always a Premonition

A premonition? The reek of alcohol
on the postman's breath
when he delivered yesterday's mail?

A premonition
always arriving before me
like an ostrich testing out its legs.

Every step it takes
marks my tardiness.
There's always a sign, a thick, greasy feather
plucked from a regal plume.

By accident
you wipe away my kisses
along with your shaving cream, there, by your ears.
A premonition... another premonition.
I ought to be more careful. Ants grow restless
when the dampness sets in. Always a premonition...
I'm tired of the daily routines,
a vacuum cleaner wiping away dust
breathing in tomorrow's unpredictability
black wire wound round my leg.

Test

Tested at every turn
like a noun
in declension.

so true

In the existential ablative
nails sprout from my imagination
like case endings aligned
by my dead cells.

In the genitive
I chase the dwarf
who stripped off my chain
of lymphocytes
dried out by the moon.
And in the dative I'm quiet
bending over myself
crushing parasites at night
in the encampments.

Whereas in the nominative and accusative
I am Narcissus, naked.
Someday, alone,
I'll drown in my own
dreams.

So Long As

So long as we still reflect each other –
even deformed – as through silver spoons,
wine glasses, and exultant bottles
on the table of a dinner party about to begin,
things can't be that bad.
But, eventually, steam
rolls in through the kitchen door
like a ghost without a soul
and then...
and then...

With a Piercing Clarity

You complain that your shoulders grow cold
that you cannot stay naked till midnight.
Lust clings to the dark sides of our bodies.

The yellow lampshade clicks off
and darkness swallows light
like a starfish consuming black prey
in its muscular belly.
I hear only the rhythmic breathing
of a smouldering fire
licking its pink bones.
The dried-up leaf of timidity crumbles
circles rotate over our faces like crossed eyes...
Fear in its postmodern form
is similar to what we had once known –
the clarity of the window
we stood in front of
before the hungry images shattered.

Over the icy magma of your grey curiosity

Over the icy magma of your grey curiosity
I stride barefooted so I can feel every change
and it hurts.
I feel a wilted palm sprout between my shoulder-blades
like uncertain lightning between sheepfolds.
I feel a cold eye, a shrew's burrow under water,
a fear that remains a chain of mute consonants.
It blows across us yet there is no wind.
We are like sails lowered in good weather.

A heart nailed to a door is a red lantern
illuminating only those who leave.
What emanates from inside is our demise –
grass spreading over the rib cage
of an old metal-frame chest.

Frost

Predictably, the first frost arrived
simplifying what we saw.
The atmosphere began to hibernate
into the realm of hypothesis.

First you touched the inviting flora of my eyes
then the untrodden earth
with its subtle memory of grain
(my fingers now held tight).
Then, after the clay, you touched upon
our ancient apprehensions, irresponsibility,
vengeance for a story left untold.

And on and on until you reached a layer of water.
Can you hear it flowing?
This is my vivid core, you can't go any deeper.
And yet you do... further and further. We were wrong.
Here the elemental world of cold metals begins –
here identity, weight, gravitational forces end,
where I can no longer be I.

Frost arrived, the scene sufficiently simplified
the sound of an accordion, roads cordoned off,
breath freezing at the first syllable
turning to beautiful coral
transforming into coral.

The Bed

My bed, a temple
where murmurs of a stifled prayer press
against my palate.

Frozen genitalia
buried fruit, imperfect fruit
clean green leaves stretching out beneath the blankets

to reach you, your warmth
dew on the skin of a morning dream.
A mole like a coffee bean on your back
arms that rarely hold me
and my eyes, rocks of salt
brought ashore by the tide.

My bed is not a bed, but a temple:
we change sheets as often
as the religious replace candles.
We leave our shoes in a neat row outside the door.
The heads of sacrificed birds roll up the stairs
to where we are throbbing, a single being split in half
martyred by silence.

Absence

The moon
nicotine of a kiss...

A sideways glance
like the mast of a pirate ship
beyond a distant island.

Silence

You and I
and two empty coffee cups

and some fugitive word
struggling in a spider's web
to save its life.

Twenty nails
lie on the table
like shells spilled
from a child's torn pocket
onto asphalt.

Outside
the morning air
chews its leftovers.

Our eyes remain
fixed on the empty cups
shapes of distant cosmos
drowning in sediment...

A shadow stretches its body
along the wall
and douses the candle's flame

a flame lighting two thin wrists
poorly bandaged wrists.

Our Words Have Grown Old

Our clothes have worn out
our shoes leak
speech grows old...

We look into each other's eyes
swallow cold food
and once in a while a word
trembles in the air
like the feathers of a bird
with its head chopped off.

Frail Bones

Why are you calling me?
What can I do for you now?
What can I do for the voice shaking like a cut wire
saying, 'I am exiled,
and have nothing left but a pen-and-paper coffin...'

Dismal thoughts cross my mind –
hunchbacked, presumptuous, slammed
like empty kettles against
the army's kitchen wall.

What do you want from me at this hour?
The water around you has receded
and you are ugly as a desert gorge,
as the moon's potbelly hanging over a glacier.

This is what happens
when you give nothing of yourself
when you kiss a pregnant woman
you never intend to marry.
Your eyes are red
as putrid meat
from your withered shoulder-blades
hangs a rattlesnake
(umbilical cord that
feeds you nothing but air).

I am evicted;
like the stone of the Chinese Oracle
my feeble soul
cannot fit into its cube-shaped house.

Truth

Truth is always someone else's privilege.
Lock your doors until it passes over you
as the Jews did in Egypt.
If it reaches your mouth, don't be merciful.
Chew it up like a piece of liver
and force it to withdraw into your own bitterness.
If you try to spit it out
I'll be there to scold you
my curses isolating you more each day
your broad bare shoulders forlorn as basilicas.

So recently banished, we keep stopping to ask
why we are here, why we were born
covered with a single leaf
molded by a potter's filthy palm.

Were we always looking for a clean body to lean on –
Could this be a story of thistles
left to soak in the sunlight?
Let me touch you. There is only one real truth:
that which the hand feels.
The rest is white mist
rising from a Turkish bath
hovering into eternity.

Truth is someone else's privilege.
Don't you know that by now?
We could never have borne
the loneliness of water
could never have balanced
like two stone angels on the lip of a fountain.

The Blossoming Almond Branch

You never know when love will reappear
like an eagle above the sea
tracing us with a deep penetrating gaze.

It may come when old age has knocked us down
and the smallest shock will undo us.
It will be painful to face in the morning
when with all its grandeur sunlight
unfolds upon a blossoming almond branch
arched over a crumbling wall.

And the sun will never reach its zenith.
Like a pumpkin it grows horizontally
dreaming under the green leaves of a garden.

It's exactly here where we first met.
You were a sealed white envelope.
If I came any closer to you
wax would stick to my chest
and the message would be lost forever.

Look at that hand with its slim and delicate fingers
spread on the wall, that morning ray.
It's not a challenge to us. It reaches out in generosity.

And the roads that will lead you to Alaska
awaken. The wooden signs left behind at barred mines
struggle to recall the damaged syllables, to remember
coal cars emerging from the warm underworld.

Still Life

Here in a summer full of dust
the dampness of winter
trails us into dark corners.

I bought the shoes days ago
but they remain untouched in the box
heel to heel.

Blessed is the sunbeam that falls upon us
like the eye of a stranger focused on a *natura morte*.
A platter of the season's finest fruit
so plump, and nestled among it, a shiny dagger.
It's not dangerous
but as alluring and peaceful
as the fruit that surrounds it.

What has become of us?
My hands, skilful and transparent,
slice the atmosphere into rabbit feed.

Another new pair of shoes
to help you enjoy a stroll around the grounds.
Since you've left I dream of only one thing:
the sound they would make
in the evening
as you reach the front door.

The Habitual

The wind slashes its own face.

The cold metallic glare
of a broken needle
in the rough coat of speech.

On a thunderbolt's edge
teeth are sharpened...

At night my dreams quake
the bed with their incestuous love-making.
They have the same blood type
but won't recognise each other in the morning.

Tracks along a wet floor...
I'll wake when the sad dog's paw
scratches the door
at midnight.

Within Another Idiom

I could have been born in another place
within another idiom
and stood beside another
in perfect harmony, or in utter chaos.
If only I could be reborn
and drift between bald dolls and my parents' hands –
different parts of the selfsame boat.
A woman's steely voice hovers above me
but I am a chestnut wrapped in green thistle
ripening under the feet of exhausted pedestrians.

I ought to wear my old sweater again
the one the colour of a hepatitis-stricken sun
and reread love letters from schoolboys
their round, fleshy syllables mushrooming off the page.
I ought to listen more closely to the sound the wind makes
scampering against a narrow pane of glass.

And, all the while, the scent of rosemary, rosemary
the consolatory rosettes blossoming on walls...

Like a Moslem cloak – a cloak wound round me
several times, round my bosom, oh my bosom
pitch-black valleys – the innocence
            of the world could suffocate me.

But, at last...
I can only hope for any laceration
any tear in the nylon net which gathers us together
and drags us along
until the moment our bodies, covered in scales
feel the dry burn of salt.

Betrayed

Betrayed woman, like an outgrown shirt
like the worn hole on an old belt
like a starched collar...
Betrayed woman, who wakes from nightmares
feeling like dirt in the corner of an eye
like a kettle taken off the stove
still steaming.

Her hips sway rhythmically
in a chewing motion
as she moves diagonally through the house.
The children, oh the children, bubbling forth!
Late at night, an aluminium lid
above a sprig of parsley –
limp nerve floating in a cold lemony broth.

There is a betrayed man, too,
betrayed by dark angels
with shoulders covered in ferns.

Betrayed men and women
accept fate nobly
as one would accept a murky glass of water
at a rest stop along the way.
Betrayed men and women
on a long journey.

III

Once Again About My Father

Forgive me, father, for writing this poem
that sounds like the creak of a door
against a pile of rags
in a room with cobwebs in its armpits
a cold so bitter it stops your blood.

The same old black-and-white television
deformed images in its chest
the same old threadbare bedspread
like the face of a menopausal woman.
Next to a lamp, Adam's shrivelled apple,
a hunger in your washed-out eyes.

You remember to ask me about something
when a toothpick snaps between your teeth.

I know how it is with you now, father:
by now you are content with loneliness –
its corpse in minus four degrees centigrade
its aluminium siding
its brace of dust
its calm sterility, infinitely white.

The Moon in November

The moon in November.
Lightning sucks
the warm blood of summer.

A bell
tolled by the deaf-mute.

The winds make love
in rusted cans.

A memory –
the scarecrow's sleeve
draped
over cut stalks.

The moon
an antique brass coin
that can only be traded
for a drunkard's iris.

The moon in November
a throat rising and lowering
to the tune of rumination.

Only the Beginning

Alas, here is the small airport covered in frost
and here the plane that takes off
leaving it behind the way a chipped tooth abandons a boxer.

That town remains behind forever
with its new and dry bridges
resembling women gone astray
its many churches a flock of eagles
watching out over a singular abyss.
The house with two gates
covered in late August rain
my euphoric steps upon its wooden floor
synchronised with the hammering
of a man who abhors the concept of time.
He taught me to hold fast to my skin
as the darkness holds up walls
in a building under construction.

The plane emerges from a large barren cloud
and old men slumber in it
like half-whitewashed trees.

Further along, the plane flutters amid mysterious air pockets
and my body crackles like a handful of twigs in winter.
It's the fox that holds fast to its old den
it's the spirit that returns at dawn. Here everything begins...

Yearly Snow

In this city the yearly snow
leaning on sparse, lonesome trees
doesn't mean a thing.
It signifies nothing more
than the meandering of a veteran
leaning on a wooden crutch.

The same war story told a hundred times
the same brand of cigarette distributed by friendly hands
and those same eyes hovering, dark and lazy.
Only that. And the dry rhythmic knocking
until his silhouette disappears
amidst the shadows cast down by rooftops
their melting snow dripping
in terrible slowness...

Chronic Appendicitis

How odd this winter is.
A felled tree in a forest
hallucinates skeletons
dragged out of the body.

Wet kisses on a bed of wet leaves
the shudder of a notary's hand
curving symmetrically against a sky
covered in paper and glue.

The inner light of things would be enough
to fuel our chlorophyll
for we are as free as germs...
we are frail trees, gracious plants,
half our bodies
bent in the wind.

The exhalation of cars in traffic
the exhalation of a dying February:
carbon dioxide creaking forth from lungs
like bedsprings in an orphanage.

February's edict slowly expires
and again rain, rain, and more rain –
rain moaning under the excruciating suffering
of chronic appendicitis
rain without thunder, without lightning.

Half Past Three

Half past three. The hour when all matter
separates into cause and effect.
My bed floats in the shallow waters of a lagoon
its legs cast in bronze
gripping the carpet.

An axe strikes rhythmically
against the sequoia trunk
of world harmony.
The same old history
no winners or losers...

The beginning and the end, both cryptic and vague:
two midwives pushing cruelly at my belly. Nearby,
like a burnt-out log
a cat, bored of being stroked,
dozes on its paws.

Half past three in the morning, my elements break down
into air, water, fire, earth,
until I am unrecognisable.

I am not my own enemy. My enemy is the light.
And the Yellow River of China.
With the tragic history
of bridges arching over it.

On a Night Like This

On a night like this lightning
bounds unexpectedly across fields of corn.
Thunder, ghost of a stampeding herd,
flashes black and white on celluloid
the stench of dirt and flesh
ready to escape
its own silhouette.

Restless as two mountain ranges
we dream the same dreams:
small, white clouds pissing
like little boys behind the school wall.

The Awakening of the Eremite

All ideas escape me
one by one, secretly slipping away
like witnesses to a political crime.

When they crawl back, tortoise-slow
the air trembles nervously in its wheelchair
and I rise.

My shadow, liberated, wanders
the room on an invisible cord
gravity sudden as a dead fly
dropped from a spider's nest.

All ideas escape me –
how far this time I cannot say.
Perhaps they'll turn up in a train station somewhere
in a town where they are unwelcome.

Outside, the moon presses against the hills
like a prophet's tongue against his palate.

The walls, protesting,
return my voice two, three, four times over
an echo horribly replicating itself
while slowly inside me
the eremite awakens.

The Almshouse

In the yard, between the stones
grass withers
beneath the weight of a walking stick.

Inside, dentures float
in glasses of water
like bottled messages
that will never be read
drifting in a rising sea.

Antipastoral

If only there could be three more snowfalls
before clouds descend upon the green mountains
and the forest's suffering reemerges from beneath tree bark.

From radios the name 'Aisha' echoes meaninglessly,
an oval foreboding turning like an oriental bracelet around a dark ankle.
Local inhabitants speak of the now legendary Red Fox.

The fires doze... hunters clean their guns.
Tomorrow will be a fine day for a chase.
At dusk they'll return with torches that shudder like quails,
shaking the moon's white cubes off their boots.

Meanwhile worms burrowing into wood
make a ceaseless grating sound
oblivious of the hasty prayers of those seated around the table.
And the wind howls in vain, to no end,
like a senile dog on the kitchen floor, licking its calves
while eyeing a string of red jalapeño peppers.

Out of Boredom

Out of boredom
roebucks lie down with toads
night swallows the moon
like a sleeping pill
and sky becomes lace
on the veil of a dreamer.
A white strand of smoke rises
like a cypress
from a burning cigarette.

The clock tower warbles a soldier's old tune
the one he whistles as he polishes his steel crutches.
An old woman's fingers, anxious as a child's
held out for a nickel, tap a tarot card.

Out of boredom
footsteps consume the streets
with the hunger of Chaplin in a silent film.
Out of boredom the soul, like an amoeba,
expands and divides
so that it will no longer be alone.

Heathen Rejoicing

Your lips
rugged as a cliff
a cliff hunched over the geometric plane
of my conscience
drawn taut to breaking.

From the depths of the Bible
our clay statues awaken
to complete the cycle of love and loneliness.
Your mouth on the screen
a black hole –
anti-time.

We worship our graven images
clay statues
earthen idols
so that we can turn the clocks back
to times of innocence
the heathen rejoicing.

Quite by Accident

Regardless
I recognised your face
struck by the car's green grille.
I felt
and smelled
in the desert wind
your face, your hand
along my spine.
A clock spring broke
and I wailed
like a bucket hitting the bottom
of a dried-up well.

But now I know we are strangers
and happen to have passed one another quite by accident
like two photographs
on the front page of the daily newspaper.

Self-defence

Confined
to a tent of soldiers
who will never return home.
If you try to leave
you will step on the bodies
sleeping beside you.

You have nowhere to go.
The stars
those witches' fingernails
stir your destiny through the fog.

In the corner
among ashes
you count the holes in your old blanket.
You breathe in bits of everyone's dreams.
Like an iceberg you ignore all borders.

While in your blood
surprisingly enough
the leucocytes multiply.

No Time

You asked for death, you were tired.
You asked for it so easily
as if calling for the white horse
with a bag of oats.
You did not know your destiny lay
in a bullet, dripping with blood,
extracted from your body.

It was December 1950.
The murder notice
blackened newspapers like a rotted tooth.
The river froze to a razor's edge
olive trees nearly snapped
beneath the weight of their dark fruit.

Death came silently, without a grave.
We were even afraid of your body.
On my palms were bloody scratches, thorny roses.
I did not know where to hide them.

You died during the revolution.
There was no time to bury you.
You left simply, as quietly as those moments when
wearing a decrepit soldier's coat
we wait on a platform for the next train.

In the Home of the Dead Man

In the home of the dead man
the lights stay on till midnight
like toppled sand dunes
beneath a red sky
a flock of blackbirds.
A felt hat left behind
by the last visitor
coffee rank
as the darkened armpits
of men wearing white shirts.
With the greatest ease this afternoon
we launched a boat into black waters
and cried: 'Swim!'

In the home of the dead man
a bed is missing.
So is a wooden stake from the yard –
details nobody has noticed.
Gone too are the stars
the shepherd once with his crook
drove across the sky
to keep them away
from gardens and houses.

Night Landscape

An anaconda of suspicion
twists through
this endless night.

A moonbeam treads
blindly over the bed
like King Edyp's hand.
My fingers touch
the sleeping baby's hair.
Oh, Lord, how coarse
the roots churned up
by my body's erosion.

Like tattoos on a pirate's arm
anguish is drawn terribly
on faces.

Perhaps later I will sleep
and night's ebb
will embrace me in its salty profundity
like a lost shoe
washed ashore.

King Edyp: Oedipus, in Albanian.

Farewell, Sunny Days

He who checked out yesterday
had the look of an amnesiac
and a little sand in the small lock of his suitcase.

Tomorrow it's my turn
to return the key, still warm, to the reception desk
my skin stripped down, yet somehow thicker.
I'll leave behind the remnants of a tired soul
the way one might leave change for the waiter
dressed in white shirt and black bow tie.

Farewell warm days, sunny days
in white shirt
and black bow-tie.

Watching Them Nap

When I lay you down my darlings
in the foggy drowsiness of a hot afternoon
dozing lightly
you are two white Mediterranean villages
under a grey sky.

The breath of my little girl
the twinkling of a barley field
mingles with my nicotine breath –
strands of blonde hair
on the weathered shoes of a barber.

Saturday evening is smooth
as a porcelain bath
from whose water a knee emerges
and sometimes a white elbow –
stars that survived the night.

My shadow drifts through the rooms
with my eternal anguish
watching you, my loves,
as I would watch anything innocent in this world.

And when one day you come to understand this
your pasts will converge into a single instant
all calm ending with a short cutting whistle
like the last drops of water
whirling down the tub's metal drain.

A Mutual Understanding

(for Lea)

I can't escape your sunflower-gaze.
Do not judge me for what I lack –
a mother's instinct
which like a water bottle grown cold
ends up at the foot of the bed.

Understand me: we are alike, you and I,
yielding to the everlasting intricacies
between two people.
Like you
I too think of our lives as a thing without history
an apple you bite once
then throw away without remorse.

Half-Cubism

Mosquitoes stick to the wet paint
on the portrait in which I am still
twenty years old. Dusk rubs up against
the run-down factory railing
like a heifer scratching its back.

And nowhere else can people
be found taking such pride
in their descendance from clay
as here at the seaside.
The moon relieves its bladder
in the last romantic corner
between concrete block buildings
packed tight with anxiety.

Across the road a disco
swells with lights
rumbles like a gorilla pounding its chest
trying impossibly to say 'I love you...'
And the yellow grass whispers with relief
as a blond boy returns from a casual fuck
alone through the darkening field.

Seasons Change

As seasons change
windows darken
coffee stains the corners of lips.
The old rusty stars
wipe clean off the body.

As seasons change
the trees wail
their shadows swelling over the river

the worms rehabilitated
the flies and birds repatriated
maggots and snakes deported to their homeland

and along the border we wait pale-faced
fake passports in our hands.

The green breath of sheep at the slaughteryard
the purple breath of bells unpondered
invades the air.
Ghosts emerge bleached white
from dark corridors
like stilts in the rain.

We line up at bus stations
the schedules unchanged
the cloud formation incestuous and ashamed
constricting above the barren hills.

Seasons change
rhythmically and without fail
like guards at the great institution
crossing through the trapezoidal shadow
cruel and grey.

CHILD OF NATURE

I

Winter Prelude

Darkness has not yet fallen
and from a neighbour's yard
comes a hammer's pounding –
the apiary mended for winter's hibernation.
What good is it knowing who switched off the light?
It's better not to see that face.
Let the last mouthful of light devour itself.
Let the door of the coal stove
enjoy the fading purple glow.
You are old enough
to sit close by with a black poker.
When the room cools down
we both dream of the gypsy woman
the rattling of her silver earrings
her full breasts, and her premonition:
a blue-eyed woman
the birth of six children.

Narration in the Third Person

It begins
when she searches in the darkness
for her likeness, a line of verse awaiting its end rhyme
or for a little music, or the exchange of carbon dioxide between
       flowers in the evening
the feeling of turning forty.
And it is just a matter of style
the manner in which she finds herself
because no clashes, no noise at all is expected any longer
the hardest hits already taken
like a statue that's lost its nose.

A forty-year-old woman
is a shadow in search of an object
a voice in the third person, a series of lessons
with little notes written in red, underlined
along the right margin. The space between lines is flesh, is someone
in the waiting-room behind a dentist's door
where the stench of arsenic
comes and goes.
Experience, experience, experience!
Little zigzags and a sense of accomplishment
with which the silkworm gnaws the mulberry leaf
starting from the tip.

She makes peace with everything: she keeps her drawers tidy,
practises yoga,
the takeoffs and landings
on the runway of her soul.

When she approaches forty
or better yet, *if* she approaches forty,
because being forty isn't required
it's her choice
like choosing a park bench
that faces away from the street
waiting for no one in particular.

Monday in Seven Days

1

Monday feels like an odd shoe
its other chewed by the dog tied at the gate.
The sun always rises through the open backdoor
and pours into the house like birdfeed along the street.
Men returning from the pebble beach
walking with their hands held behind them
on their way to nowhere
look like crosshairs on a gun
their spit still bitter with coffee
dandruff scattered along their collars;
to draw them you would have to hold your breath.
For weeks now there hasn't been a single drop of rain. The thin
                    stream dwindles, sickly, syphilitic.
A child skipping school
sneaks away from his mother.
He is nine and still adds and subtracts on fingers
                    blackened by fresh walnuts
counting the years to his conscription.
He draws a large dusty circle in the dirt
that looks like a piece of blighted flesh
where a tumour had just been removed.

2

Like salmon, ready to mate,
swimming upstream from the sea
to the river's estuary
the wedding guests step backward in time
and beg the landlady to return their flesh:
'Mine is bright white...'
'Mine is soft, with a burn from a hot iron on my forearm...'
'Mine smells of sage, like a canvas bag...'
'Mine is magical, you can wear it inside out...'
'Give me anything – it doesn't matter!'

Here comes Mustafa, the drunkard,
with his head stuck to his body's right side.
He is Monday's Saint, guilty of everything,
absorbing everyone's sins
like a swab of alcohol-dabbed cotton
pressed to a wound.

3

Before sleep the world returns whole beneath eyelids
like an army full of pride, gathered under the Arc de Triomphe,
the loot of war behind them.
The nightly rite of fucking
that shredded music
sufficient to hide
the motive for which we woke up this morning
and, even more so, the motive to wake up tomorrow.

The lamp turns off for the last time
and blood continues on its small circular route.

4

When my grandma came here as a bride
with nothing more than her good name
the house was empty but for the hanging weapons.
There was so little here she had to build a whole town
just to find a pair of shoulders for a head.
She began by planting an apricot tree in front of the house
and later another, so that the two were
like hands cupped to a face
to warm it.
Then children dripped from her
as rain from a tin awning.
Those who fell on soft ground were forgotten.
Those on cement
managed to survive.

To this day
they still stand petrified in a black and white photograph
in woollen suits with oily unevenly cut hair
looking uncomfortable
looking as if their lives were borrowed from elsewhere.

5

Broken toys were my playthings:
zebras, wind-up Chinese dolls, ice-cream carts
given to me as New Year's presents by my father.
But none was worth keeping whole.
They looked like cakes whose icing had been
                licked off by a naughty child

until I broke them, cracked and probed their insides, the tiny
                                gears, the batteries,
not aware then that I was rehearsing
                my understanding of freedom.

———

When I first looked at a real painting
I took a few steps backward instinctively
                on my heels
finding the precise place
where I could explore its depth.
It was different with people:
I built them up,
loved them, but stopped short of loving them fully.
None were as tall as the blue ceiling.
As in an unfinished house, there seemed to be a plastic sheet
                above them instead of a roof
at the beginning of the rainy autumn of my understanding.

6

Here is the honest man, the just man,
his face a picnic blanket
shaken of crumbs.
His kind never remains unemployed.
He asks, 'Does anyone have a nail to drive into
the hole in my chest?'

My great-grandfather was like that,
and so was my grandfather and my father.
Maybe if I were a son I would have been the same,
staring up at a *worthless* father
(What a shame! I'd say).

'How far should I go?' the son would ask only once.
'Until you lose sight of yourself.'
It might have been a dream,
because his family tree was struck down by
                              a bolt of lightning
before the succulent scent of burnt sugar emanating from the Katsura
                              spread over the village.

7

The smell of roots in the air, and the rain falling
like bees returning to their hive, all at once.
It's a tradition in my family to distinguish happy rain from
            melancholy rain
conceived above hilltops during summer.
I listen with one ear, waiting as if for the moment one recognises
            that a stranger's voice
is indeed one's own voice.

My uncle asks for a '*fazzoletto*' to wipe his glasses.
He has used that word since the time he went to Florence
to have his pneumonia cured – a time he remembers
as fondly as a honeymoon.

With my report card in his hand
veins throb at his temples – a matter of life or death.
He is the one to determine
whether I will be a brick for a wall
or a stone for a barn.
The hand that he hits with
is an instruction manual read only once
although the furrows on his palm – the limits of his destiny –
never leave scars on me.
'To hell with it! Bring me *un fazzoletto*!'

8

'If you have dark skin
your smile is exquisite,
neither incomplete nor flashing rotten teeth.'
F. knows this. She mourns for her son.
Early in the morning she opens the window
lights the kerosene stove
with a piece of crumpled telegram still in her hand
sweeps the yard, feeds the chickens, cooks for ten,
fixes the chair with the sphinx's arms
opposite the door.
And each day
with the claws of a hawk she fights against
disorder
begging for form and discipline
like the square plots of a field of wheat
guiding the part of herself that flies mercilessly
in a straight line
never landing.

She accepts greetings with her eyes
and pathways open before her
like the Sabbath among other days,
dedicated to gratitude and prayer.

9

Medio tutissmus ibis, the middle is the safest ground.
The embroidered tablecloth in the middle of the table.
The table in the middle of the carpet.
The carpet in the middle of the room.
The room in the middle of the house.
The house in the middle of the block.
The block in the middle of the town.
The town in the middle of the map.
The map in the middle of the blackboard.
The blackboard in the middle of nowhere.

Lola is an angel. Her forehead hasn't grown since she was eight,
her centre of gravity unchanged. And she likes edges, corners,
although she always finds herself
in the middle of the bus
where people rush toward the doors at either end.

My neighbours never went to school
nor have they heard of aesthetics
and hardly ever have they read anything
about the Earth's axes, symmetry, or absolute truth.
But instinctively they let themselves drift toward the middle
like a man laying his head on a woman's lap,
a woman who, with a pair of scissors
will make him more vulnerable than ever
before the day is done.

10

Preparing for winter
isn't tradition, but instinct. We hurl our spare anxieties
like precious cargo from a shipwreck.

Taedium vitae is a time zone
that no longer exists.
The smell of boiled beans separates us
from our neighbours, a dream above the stove
separates us from our ancestors.

There isn't a middleman
between me and my talents.
The wind preaches with the nasal voice of a false prophet.
Years somersault over frozen slopes
and we instinctively hide our heads between our knees.

Limits wither away. My body
more abstract than ever, is a country without an anthem,
a country, delirious and once near death, which I touch
like a mother touching her lips to the forehead of her child
with a high fever.

The Mystery of Prayers

In my family
prayers were said secretly,
softly, murmured through sore noses
beneath blankets,
a sigh before and a sigh after
thin and sterile as a bandage.

Outside the house
there was only a ladder to climb
a wooden one, leaning against a wall all year long,
ready to use to repair the tiles in August before the rains.
No angels climbed up
and no angels climbed down –
only men suffering from sciatica.

They prayed to catch a glimpse of Him
hoping to renegotiate their contracts
or to postpone their deadlines.

'Lord, give me strength,' they said
for they were descendants of Esau
and had to make do with the only blessing
left over from Jacob,
the blessing of the sword.

In my house praying was considered a weakness
like making love.
And like making love
it was followed by the long
cold night of the body.

February Sky

Large, grey, sprawled
like an old elephant.
Winter is ending.
Low, sloping roofs are overturned boats
slumbering along the shores of drowsiness.

Twenty years of an oak tree's life
burns instantly in a stove.
And eyes meet only by accident
suburban roads
that intersect in grassy meadows
streams that swell their banks
hairs on a pillow
after a long illness.

The old elephant's hoof
tramples the ground
sewing poisonous yellow flowers
in its path
flowers without scent.

Yellow Book

In times without truth there are no taboos.
Maybe this yellow book is one of a few that survived
although the act of hiding it
lives on in our minds.

In the scorching heat, dinner is served clumsily every night
at the same hour, the hour when light and dark cover us equally.
Something is quickly cooked; a calf's head perhaps, of which I'll
        get the tongue.
They say that if you eat it your tongue will grow
and if you eat the eyes you will be a sharpshooter
and if you eat books you will eat yourself
little by little, from the edges to the center,
like tractors harvesting at collective farms.

From the head of the table, the head of the family
fingers his warts while lecturing on evolution:
'The strongest die, the weakest survive.'

Nothing distinguishes this from a holy dinner
where food and wine are portioned out equally –
only the truth is read secretly
by the mystified, sharing it
like a yellow book.

Yellow books were books banned under the Communist regime. [Tr.]

Country Roads

In the country, fate steps
softly, never rushes anywhere
traverses the crucifixes
of cart tracks in the dirt.

A chimney exhales rings of smoke
and the sky's black fingers twirl them
across the blind milky way.

Through the iron bars
of a little pub window
light spills out in white rectangles
like playing cards
overturned on a dusty table.

The nightwatchman's dog
sits on a rickety chair
wagging its tail,
drooling, belching at stars.

And the shingle-covered roofs
clustered together in groups of four or five
resemble the scaly backs of crocodiles
drifting downriver
making sounds
not unlike drowning men.

Old News

In the village nestled between two mountains
the news always arrives one month late,
cleansed in transit, glorified, mentioning only the dead who made
      it to paradise,
and a coup d'état referred to as 'God's will'.

Spring kills solitude with solitude, imagination
the sap that shields you from your body. Chestnut trees
awaken, drunken men
lean their cold shoulders against a wall.

The girls here always marry outsiders and move away
leaving untouched statues of their fifteen-year-old
selves behind.

But the boys bring in wives
from distant villages,
wives who go into labor on heaps of grass and straw in a barn
and bear prophets.
Forgive me, I'd meant to say 'only one will be a prophet'.
The others will spend their lives throwing stones
(that is part of the prophecy, too).

At noon on an autumn day like today
they will bolt out of school like a murder of crows stirred by the
      smell of blood
and chase the postman's skeleton of a car
as it disappears around a corner, leaving only dust.

Then they will steal wild pears from the 'bitch's yard'
and nobody will stop them. After all, she deserves it. She's sleeping
      with two men.

Between the pears in one boy's schoolbag
lies a copy of *Anna Karenina*.
It will be skimmed over, impatiently, starting on the last page
cleansed and glorified, like old news.

In a Nameless Place

No need to fill in a form
or to tap your fingertips with annoyance.

No need to do anything
in a place run by ghosts –
the temple stones lugged from afar, perhaps as far as a kilometre –
to taste the geometry of shadows.

The doors are open because there's nothing to steal
from the city-state of diseased poets.
Like bandages on scuffed eyebrows
the postboxes open only when wet.

A town without advertisements, without pretty women
selling cavity-free smiles, without streets pointing to the suburbs,
the limits of cognition – the dictatorship of a blade of grass.
I greet my neighbours, but they don't return the favour.
What's the point of wishing someone good luck
when one is born and dies in a single day, perhaps within an hour?

Here they all are! On my worktable,
on the backs of books, little photos,
with the garden of Eden gleaming in the background,
stuck like receipts to the neatly hung clothes at the drycleaner's.

And finally, astonishingly, I don't know how to name this place.
A nation without martyrs doesn't have a name.
Deserters, yes, are branded, as Spartan deserters once were,
with half-shaved faces –
light and darkness come together.

Regarding Hypermetropia

Don't blame me for losing the ability to see what's near.
A bay with no harbour,
I grew up without being kissed on the forehead at bedtime.
I never heard cryptic footsteps beneath my window
and no one whispered in my ear.
The olive grove in my yard was state-owned
and looked like armour riddled by bullets; even after a bumper crop
not a single olive reached our table.
Never has a glass, bearing the impression of my lips,
shattered. Maybe it was because of superstition
but dishes were washed instantly, and never broke.
Never have I rummaged through a drawer
that didn't give a slapped puppy yelp.
And never have I seen the flickering of a nightdress
gliding stealthily between rooms
nor felt the warmth of things that were solely mine –
the banister that led to my floor of dreams –
things belonging to me and things I belonged to.
My strength never came from the inside
but from the outside,
smoked meat
at the mercy of salt and frost.

Never have I savoured the sweet taste of blame
nor the tartness of repentance
portioned out like halva
at a requiem.

Waiting for a Poem

I'm waiting for a poem,
something rough, not elaborate or out of control,
something undisturbed by curses, a white raven
released from darkness.

Words that come naturally, without aiming at anything,
a bullet without a target,
warning shots to the sky
in newly occupied lands.

A poem that will well up in my chest

and until it arrives
I will listen to my children fighting in the next room
and cast my gaze down at the table
at an empty glass of milk
with a trace of white along its rim
my throat wrapped in silver
a napkin in a napkin ring
waiting for late guests to arrive....

For Attention

My daughter laughs at how I choose which clothes to wear
at how I keep my hair pinned to one side
like a little girl in white stockings
waiting anxiously for someone
to push her swing.
Others laugh at how I walk
or sleep on my stomach, or eat with one hand....
I too laughed at my mother
when she came to the parent-teacher conference
with her hair still wet
coffee stains on the corners of her lips
her dumpy clothes, thick gnarled stockings,
an old-fashioned necklace with an amulet
turned yellow from sunlight.

And today, here we are, she and I, like two sides of the same yard –
one in the front, the other in the rear.
We seek attention differently, she and I:
she like a dervish sticking pins under her skin
and I
crumpling the wrapper of a chocolate.

You're One of Us

Among seven days, eight are faded out
like the armpits and chests of denim work clothes.
You're one of us!

Among seven women, eight have swollen varicose veins
and kidneys wrapped tight with woollen sashes.
You're one of us!

The youngest imitates her mother's pain, hands on waist
trying to gain her acceptance.
You're one of us!

Flitting around, with an egg in her mouth, shouting her dreams
then crushing them with stones, like dwindling fires lit by children.
You're one of us!

Either scorn or be scorned
if you are a seed that doesn't lay roots.
But when I produced scorn like a penknife out of my pocket
it failed to cut:
'Watch out! You'll cut your hands! Put that thing away!'
You're one of us!

Homonymic lives, all of ours,
mine no exception
misery that old typewriter
with its accent key missing.
You're one of us!

Me, one of them
and in two places simultaneously.
I, the premonition of another life.

Waiting for a Witness

Nonsense! Why would you wait for something created out of
      nothing?
Despite the washed and pressed sheets
the sterilised scalpel, iodine, the basket of biological vowels
and the nightshift doctor napping on a chair
like a landlady waiting for her husband
to come back empty-handed from hunting,
my autogenetically born child still wails.
My body, as if aimed by catapult at a disinfectant-sprayed wall
finds it difficult to be indoors
to awaken the distaste of three generations
and its only motive is continuity, hostage-taking, and a political cause
tricky as the screech of a night owl that awakens an avalanche.
A window slams shut; tobacco gardens bend
in awe toward the soul that first shaped despair.
Now comes more crying.
Behold which grandmother or great-grandmother of mine fell into
      that trap
which one chose my daughter's body
as a witness: what she saw, heard, or touched
and more importantly, what she thought – but a witness isn't
      allowed to think
after swearing herself in on the battered book of truth
with an illiterate hand.

The Wanderings of Freedom

Not always does the plague of the first born
pass over the doorway architrave
smeared with blood.

Does the powerful and irreversible tempest drive away
those who believe they are destined for the Promised Land?
And does it divide them along the way?

I remember when I was ten
my happy, restless wanderings,
a spoon beating white meringue.

I felt my soul radiating
from my warm body,
fragrance from blossoming night flowers.

That wasn't freedom. Freedom wasn't a feeling of spaciousness.
Freedom was a vertical ascension
sacks of sand hauled by hot air balloons –
a sacred suspension!

I shake these memories from my body
as a zealot would shake dust from a carpet
whose arabesque wakes him from a dreamy sleep.

At last I am free from the illusion of freedom.
Now I am free.

Prisoners

Prisoners
guilty or not
always look the same when they are released –
patriarchs dethroned.

This one just passed through the gate
head bowed despite not being tall
his gestures like a Bedouin's
entering the tent
he carried on his back all day long.

Cotton curtains, stone walls, the smell of burnt lime
take him back to the moment
the cold war ended.

The other day his sheet was hung up in the courtyard
as if to flaunt the blood stain
after a wedding night.

Faces tarnished by sun
surround him, all eyes and ears:
'What did you dream of last night?'
A prisoner's dreams
are parchment
made sacred by its missing passages.

His sister is still discovering his odd habits:
the bits of bread hidden in pockets and under his bed
the relentless chopping of wood for winter.

Why this fear?
What can be worse than life in prison?

Having choices
but being unable to choose.

They Hasten to Die

They are dying one after the other;
shovelling earth on them has become as common
as sprinkling salt on food.

They all are of the same generation, my family,
or more accurately, of one era,
and the children of an era are like dogs tied to a sled:
in their search for gold
they either run together or fall together.

It is not mathematics,
but more like combs, combs which tame any hair's rebellion
after a mad flirtation before a mirror.

The Forgotten

The words we speak do not tell linear stories –
they are our living fossils.
Cats, unlike us, are all instinct,
their escape routes written in black and white
in arrows, crosses, and dashes.

Some say the morning birds, not cats or dogs, absorb
the whole day's warmth. I absorb the energy
of people close to me
as cats do.
A pure energy
with no electrons to exchange
the energy of an ice cube dazzling in a glass–
the energy of people thinking aloud
exchanging ideas.

My people do everything loudly.
They suffer loudly; even their silence is loud.
Their fruit always ripens too soon.

It's not heroism when at night, in secret,
the muezzin chanted verses of the Koran to us
and I lost my connection to everyone around me.
It was as if they stopped thinking
and dozed off, elbow to elbow,
like a vineyard after the harvest
no longer needing to be protected.

II

Chess

Autumn. Veins of marble
swell in the rain.

The graves of my relatives
four inches of space between them
lined up
like cars at a railroad crossing.

What once kept them together
like fingers in an ironsmith's glove
has vanished.... The war is over.

In the afterlife there are only a few strangers
waiting for the train to pass....

The smell of the earth
reminds me of home
where a clock that once hung on the wall is missing.

I polish the dust off their names with care –
the years... like little bruises on a knee,
love... which now pricks less
than the thorns of a rose.

There, at the entrance to the cemetery
the guard sits in his booth
playing chess with himself.

Self-portrait in Silica

My portrait hasn't changed much.
My head still leans a little to one side
in the same way
as if asking for an apology.
Apology? For what?
Because I was in the wrong place at the right time,
or in the right place at the wrong time,
or both? Because I was present
when asked to be invisible?
Asked not to tap a spoon against my teeth while eating, not to dream
          out loud,
not to make smoke when I get burned, not to make suds when I wash,
asked to remove my feathers when I crumble
when the elastic breaks and my soul lands between my feet
asked not to bother fixing it?
And believe me, life is light when you are invisible.
I followed the path I was told to follow.
Glass! First I was glass, full of curses, the elementary school's window
made visible by dust.
Then I was the glass of a monocle that one eye trusted and the other
          didn't.
Later, after I began to write, I became the thick glass
of a telescope
that revealed stars on the palm of a hand.
The eyes that peer through me still look tired,
and the stars, still millions of light years away.
I bear no false news, only a premonition;
my deception has distance.

Maybe someday, I won't be an invisible thing,
a winding border between two worlds.
I will have a voice, a colour, and be read on rainy days
well aware that a timid nod to a photographer
is merely an alibi.

When Love Begins To...

It enters my days arrogantly
like the silence after the clap
of a judge's mallet.

I sway in the slightest breeze
across a field of wheat
awaiting the harvest.

It arrives when I think I'm safe
when I think all I am is just a spine,
strong, without a chest or a belly,
without a navel –
like a cellar full of food
stored for winter.

I hesitate for a second
ready to start over again
with a clean painter's palette
dark fingerprint in its centre.

Then I set off on the same road
the end of which I know best:
a cold bullet bulging in my pocket
the one every good soldier saves
for the day he finds himself surrounded.

Irreversible Landscapes

Irreversible is the river
on whose back
dead leaves swirl.
Irreversible are words –
the dust of roads
mingled with breath, warm breath
that sticks to our trembling lips
like fog to a boat.

Irreversible is this cup of tea
irreversible the restrained aura of melancholy
after a superficial conversation
about books and cemeteries.
Perhaps even routine –
the eggcup
that keeps half of our round selves
in balance –
is irreversible.

Irreversible are all moments of love
even when they happen more and more frequently
even when skin turns to moss.
In love two bodies become one cactus
fused always
to that instant of death.

Particularly in the Morning

In the morning, particularly in the morning,
my body stretches out, each part distinct, formless,
like a gun dismantled on a tablecloth.

Yesterday is volcanic stone
perfection itself
nothing to add or remove.

And then there's him, lying on his side,
clay that can be shaped in endless ways.
'Is it time for coffee?'

And although he is still sleeping
with the face of a stranger, the face of sleep,
a face without memory,
it is he and only he who knows my body's code
that flows like a river by a colony of gypsies
unaware of its source or estuary.

The White Stain

My head on your left shoulder
is a zero valence – a grey metallic loneliness.
Freckles, spots of rust...
Time drips slowly, mercury in the thermometer
hung on the wall shyly slides away
 – autumn's striptease
revealing what was hidden.

Each night, the same nightmare.
The silkworm
gnaws at fresh leaves
and your shadow slips from the chair
like a low-cut evening dress
I once wore.

Your zero valence is
a hopeless chemical loneliness –
burning flesh,
black suffocating gases.

Unconditional love
has always frightened me –
as has the stewardess in white, there, near the exit
who directs us to fasten our seatbelts
near the end of the journey.

The Island

You and I
live on an island
far from cities with traffic lights and people.

Outside we hear the rustlings
of a bed of reeds
where the wind with its toothless mouth blows
luring in tides.

A boat is moored on the shore
a forlorn boat
rotting in the rain.

It seems
we'll never be able to use it
to sail home.

A Pair of Sandals Under a Tree

That was it.
Now body, breath, and tree are one.
Tree? What tree? There's no tree beyond the window
no tree to crave
the tranquillity of bodies washed ashore.

A little courage is all I need
to open my eyes and confront
the fearful scene before me –
the moon at midday
coming into focus in the dome of the sky.

Sometimes my belly contracts
like a cobra
that just swallowed its prey.
Yours rises and falls, without pause, never understated,
inclusive as a manifesto.

Nothing could change that rhythm.
There will be little mute cracks in porcelain
dessert knives
routine things
and when wind takes shape
the death of imagination.

What tree?

Now our breathing is steady
grammatical
blades of grass and mud
in a nest recently abandoned.

We smile a little
like a pair of sandals
that expose no toes or heels
resting at the foot of a tree.

For Nights We Can Never Relive

All that has happened is
someone's conscience
has gone haywire:
our past three years, collected
in the pages of a diary,
lie scattered beneath cliffs.

Our silhouettes on the bed
look like a pair of scissors
left wide open
rusted bolt at its centre.

Your breathing: thin, quiet.
Mine: dense, troubled.
Dispersed unevenly
we are like crumbs
cast off after a rushed meal.

After the Evening Movie

Lulling in the curiosity of an evening movie
the four of us look like pieces broken off a relic,
small and large fragments
caught in an archaeologist's sieve.

Ribs, elbows, shoulders, and knees
lean freely against one another.
The illusion, flickering, reflects
off the screen onto the ionic architecture of our flesh.

'We might have been happy,' you utter
with the same compassionate tone
you use when talking about the dog tied to a pole in the courtyard
on that fearful night of lightning.
We turn out the lights, get ready for bed,
our heads glowing like lemons in the dark,
sour and dissatisfied.

'We could... if...'

We hide beneath a suffocating embrace
simply to avoid speaking
simply because we fear that we might have to tell a story
a story whose ending we don't yet know
because we no longer hear barking in the courtyard.

Clay turns on its wheel
unable to realise
that it is history itself
that same story
told over and over in countless ways.

Transit

When the limit of what you know runs circles around you
like the bubble in the compass of a little fishing schooner
that returns to the same shore each night
and you breathe in philosophy like incense
just accept it. The moment your life is replaced
with another is here –
your soul exchanged for that of a jackal
or a shark in open seas, or a butterfly balanced above an elephant's eye
or a lumberjack walking three hours
to get to the nearest pub.
At least now I know why you were always
so late.

But I'll never speak a word of thanks
for you who protected me from the unmistakable underbelly of things
feeling cold and tedious as a helmet.

Citadine Hotel, Berlin

Evening. Two or three taxis line up in a row
waiting for someone who's lost.

The room, just as I left it this morning
only the sheets have been changed
by hands I have never known
only the rain taps lightly against the window
like a withered bouquet of flowers.

The message on the answering machine is still there
the voice of a man
looking for a woman who slept here months earlier
a woman who had wiped herself dry with these same towels
clean and perfumed.

I replay it several times
piece together their past
try to avoid the question: 'What might have happened next?'

A telephone call from a phone booth
and then he arrives hurriedly and, perhaps, with great longing.
His lips wipe makeup off my face
carelessly and without pause
as the understudy does after the show.

Finally, I lie down on the bed
made by anonymous hands
stretching out among my lost words
(anxious, hurried questioning)
like a silk bookmark
between newly read pages of a book.

Understanding a Journey

Like eels reaching the sea
or elephants returning to the smooth humus of riverbanks
we embark on a long journey
to decide where to bury you.

When I die, which door
will be slammed loudest by the stormy wind?
There is no death between need and excess.
Our last bed will be but a pair of eyes.
The soul, the last to go,
separates the walnut tree
from its shadow.

Look how deeply you sleep!
The sleep of an infant
ill-fitted for old age...

The spectacles placed crosswise by the bed
are waiting for someone's breath to fog them.
Beyond their rims objects are magnified, palpable,
clear, and raw
as on the world's first day.

I am a heavy and lazy beast
digging up soil with my nails.
And if this is my last resting place
then I will never hear a twig break
hundreds of kilometres away.
The magnificent rituals of the forest in winter will continue
with an ice-cold heart
with a heart of snow.

Tango

The city has expanded
a diaphragm heaving open
a single bus stop now separating it from the cemetery.

There, seated on a stool, waits a widow, money
for a ticket clenched in her fist.
At home she cleaned herself up to her shoulders with alcohol
her body free of cuts and scratches.

Getting off the bus, she fixes her gaze on its number plate.
Her breasts, like flowers, droop
as soft rain falls like apostrophes
in a conversation between two worlds.

In winter, no one is at the bus stop
but the driver waits there habitually, the engine idling,
half a cigarette
dampened between his lips.
Soon the automatic door closes, springing back in place
like the last words of a verdict.

No one knows which expanded first,
the city or cemetery, a tango
with arms extended and thighs drawn up –
currents in open water.

A Question of Numbers

Two people form a habit.
Three people make a story.

A dog digs through the wedding trash:
Champagne bottles, cake, filets of beef, caviar,
a butchery of vows made in one night.

A castle would simply be called a 'palace'
if it weren't for the barbarian assault.

The echoes of obstacles are heard:
someone who protects you from forgetfulness,
his pain petrified.

They remember nights on the soft grave
of an anonymous Turkish soldier, making love.
His hairy shoulder was a fig leaf
trying to touch the reptilian sky
that tomorrow would slide over everyone
like a bar of soap in a public restroom.
She had freckles; he had strong instincts.
That was enough reason for them to meet again and again
without setting a fixed time.
And perhaps, he could catch that piece of sky
if she weren't so alarmed:
'Nobody's here! I want to go home!'

There is no third eye,
no self-destructive gene
to stop freedom from growing without intention
like the cancerous cells of a tumour.

The third eye will accommodate them
inside a frame, an apple bitten from both sides in their hands.
Ageing starts now.

That night, when they returned, they were only two,
less than one,
shaking off blades of grass from their bodies,
metastases of an everlasting summer.

Small Town Funeral

It always happens in the late afternoon
when the damp air stinks of oblivion
and the procession makes its way
toward a safe corner of town
like a caterpillar having just crawled
from a crack in the wall.

From a distance, women's knees flash
between skirts and stockings,
plump knees uncared for
like winter apples split in half.

And men lean their arms against the coffin
ever so gently
with no more effort
than it takes to nudge an old pot across the floor
to catch a leak.

With their free arms
they pluck oak leaves from their black suits,
clothes worn only for weddings and funerals.
And later that evening, they clean the dust and grey hairs off
with a brush and drops of vinegar
(although they may never be worn again).
And their shoes grow used to
the deafness of mud
along cemetery lanes.

I try to guess
what remains after a small town funeral.
Maybe nothing.
Not much pain, not much forewarning.
Not even wild roses or rosemary.
Only ghosts and oak leaves
humbly accepting
the gift of the first raindrops.

Shadows on the Snow

The snow comes late this year. Violet shadows
doze like shepherds around
a white fire.
The swaying shadow of a fence looks like a woman's clavicle –
a woman who dreams of her lover's journey home through the snow,
his late return.

Thin trails lead to the doorway.
A car parked for hours
compresses black earth.
Radio signals float out of earshot.
A boat with its eel fishers
in luminous raincoats skims by.
A child – his little hands trembling –
casts slanting trees across the table.

The choir kneels.
The moment has come to speak
in a voice I have never known before.

I raise my head and see a single star in the night sky
shapeless and fearful like the shard of a broken bottleneck,
a star I have for years foolishly followed.
Perhaps the shadow of my infinite persistence
looks like a large hill
on the moon, a camel bent over a puddle
preparing for a new stretch of thirst.

The Other Side of the Mountain

The peak, covered in snow
all year long,
reflects the sky, but like a dogma
never touches it.

The electrocardiogram of sweat dried in the body
spreads from shirt to shirt
contagious as a flame, infecting everyone with its slow rhythm
to the youngest in the family, a little boy
lingering like a postscript
to everything that's already been said.

But it's not hard work that sweetens the cabbage,
harvests the corn, or repairs the beehives.

It's that warm sigh, while staring at the mountain
on the other side of which
'life is, of course, better'.

The sigh is like a woman who sleeps with everybody.
Do whatever you want to her
but never ask her name
even as you leave.

Everyone here resembles each one another,
not because of incest, but because they all fuck
the same woman
who emits pheromones of the Unknown.

The Centaur constellation
highlights a narrow goat's path,
the only way out of the village.
'Goodbye,' is often heard, but never 'Welcome!'

The doors, decorated with mignonettes,
are a euphemism for the fear
that one day someone will return
to tell of what happens on the other side of the mountain.

III

Child of Nature

No one noticed me
at my parents' wedding –
my face scrunched
as if I had eaten sour fruit –
tucked away like a wet invitation in a pocket.

Soon thereafter,
my mother swung the window of her chest shut
and opened a larger one on her belly
overlooking the street
in the morning
as the scent of fresh coffee
and toast wafted in.

She knew what she desired.
I was her pure, perfect objective,
I, who humbly flew from her body –
a magpie with a diamond in its throat
a novel read aloud, beginning on the last page.

The newly opened jars of cream
in her dresser drawers
were out of bounds for me
as were the untouched perfumes and powders
lipstick the size of a finger
pointing seductively to exotic places.

I was there until the very moment
chromosomes were combined –
a handful of hazelnuts with a handful of ginger –
but not a moment later.

Vertical Realities

Waking is an obligation:
three generations open their eyes every morning
inside me.

The first is an old child – my father;
he always chooses his luck and clothes one size too small for him.

Next comes grandfather... In his day, the word 'diagnosis' did not exist.
He simply died of misery six months after his wife.
No time was wasted. Above their corpses
rose a factory to make uniforms for dockworkers.

And great-grandfather, if he ever existed,
I don't even know his name. Here my memory goes on hiatus,
my peasant origins cut like the thick and yellow nails
of field-workers.

Three shadows loom like a forest over me
telling me what to do
and what not to do.

You listened to me say 'good morning'
but it was either an elephant pounding on a piano
or the seams coming apart in my father's little jacket.

Indeed, my father, his father, and his father before that
are not trying to change anything
nor do they refuse to change anything; the soap of ephemerality
leaves them feeling fresh and clean.

They only wish to gently touch the world again
through me, the way latex gloves
lovingly touch the evidence
of a crime scene.

Men

Human existence is like a dead language
of which only an expression, a quotation, or a single word remains.

But a man without sons is a mutation.
His name will move from one ear to another by a clean female whisper
voiced like a dream without conflict
difficult to remember after night's end.

Six daughters, each birth a failure
like the gold prospector
who brings home only silk and medicinal herbs.

Without a son in the family,
there is no river to carry the toxic remains
of his black and white anger,
no one to foresee war in the bones of the pet
sacrificed for dinner;
no wars, no births or deaths
when life gets lazy in peacetime.

His cell is a cave
sketched with naive carbon drawings:
the hunter against the beast, the hunter against nature,
until the moment a woman appears around the fire.
Then strength moves from his muscles
to his eyes.
and the angle of the arrow's aim shifts.

This is the end of the ice age
the end of clarity.

There is a secret that extinguishes men from the inside
like Dwarf Stars
changing from yellow to white
and then... to black, a smudge across the cosmos.
There is no son to inherit the father's secret....
not the secret itself
but the art of solitude.

Flashback (1)

In the sweltering August of 1972
the napes of the movers' necks look green
as they load furniture onto a truck.
'Watch out! Don't step on the flowers!' my mother warns.
The flowers would whither three days later....
The house empties out as if by x-ray
and the neighbours' compassion
melts away, an ice compress
held against a wound.

We move somewhere else,
where gratitude instills itself like balconies on faces
and adventure is fixed on a stick
like a rooster-shaped lollipop.

I am only three. I do not know what promises are
and no one tells me
that a childhood without promises is bread
without yeast, still sweet yet tough and dry.

My father cannot be seen anywhere
for my father has not yet been born.
He will be born in another chapter
much later
when I begin to feel the need to be someone's protector
a little shadow growing slowly between my legs
like a microphone stand.

Flashback (2)

Heart of November. Wind blows
like a shuffling of eras.
Snow and my mother's face
wait in the background
to test their philosophy
of inevitability.
Lights, like a line of ants, lead
to the dining-room. I am the bride.
It's the end of the ceremony. And as I prepare to sleep
others carefully remove twenty-one pins from my head,
as many as the years I've lived.
I know almost nothing of life;
know only that in sharp turns
experience matters less than two burning
lights in the chest.

I try to hide my happiness under white fuzz
like an orange, carefully peeled.
I have emerged cunningly from my genetic prophecy,
holding on tight to the belly of the ram
out of the Cyclops' cave.

If I struggle to part the curtains a little
with two well-manicured fingers,
I will see two shadows moving in harmony on the asphalt
the musician and the cello after the concert:
man and the anti-prophecy.

Meditation While Shaving

Shaving *after* work? What for?
It reminds me of my father
a long time ago
standing before a mirror, cracked as
corn grits cooked without fat.
He went on shaving at that hour
a razor sliding up and down
clearing a path from temple to chin
like the words of an apostle
and as his tongue twisted like a snail
emptying one cheek and filling the other
his words rebounded from the glass:
'The power of a man, my son,
is measured by the things he doesn't do.
Passion should be kept hidden, like a turnip!'

It was as if breaking a rule, almost blasphemy
when I, years later,
early in the morning, before doing any housework
started shaving my own 'thorn bush'
using my father's razor.

When my hand trembled, I called out to God.
It wasn't difficult. It was like searching for a barber
in a familiar neighbourhood.
God is not used to saying, 'What can I do for you, young man?'
The cross is older than man.

Here I am, without a single cut
my neck lit up as if by an internal lamp.
'A clean shave,' my dad always said,
my dad whose eyes at death –
his face unshaven for days
looking like a swarm of ants
trying to lift a grain of wheat –
caved in like the crumpled napkin of a child
made to leave the table
still hungry.

A List of Things to Do

I always promise to come see you
but I never keep my promises
when they have anything to do with you

when you are just a name
on my list of things to do
always something more pressing
because you will always wait....

There's always a winter not far behind....
How difficult it must have been for you
without a glass of warm tea in the evening
tortured between cold walls
like quicksilver in mortar
now used to fill teeth.

There's always an early summer....
with the sound of your neighbour and his son
who at the strike of midnight
always come home quarrelling

while you hold a photo of a girl, cut out of the newspaper,
the atrophied song of grasshoppers in the background
chirping away until noon the next day.

Sometimes when you were no longer here
I would draw a long line across
your name on my list
beginning from the left, straight through to the right,
like the holy commandments written in the Koran
no possibility
of turning back,
father.

In the Absence of Water

It's Sunday. On the soles of shoes
walking in the hallway
snow turns to plasma, and the memories of roads disappear.

A 150-watt lamp in the middle of the room
looks like a piece of yellow cheese caught in a trap of boredom.
My mother knits, quietly counting stitches –
she always knows how many are needed, even when swapping rows.
She is stuck to her seat like putty in the corner of a window
becoming more and more clearly defined over the years.
She is a pin cushion.
She knows the art of submission instinctively
and tries to teach it to me
and my sister.
We are three matryoshka dolls lined up by size.
I am the last one –
the one that doesn't pull apart.

My Mother, the Safety Instructions, and Me

Just when I'm about to share
the discomfort of a long journey
with someone else's eyes
I notice my mother
carefully following the stewardess
perform the safety instructions
between first-class and coach.

The skin on her jaw stiffens
as she prays to her gods.

I try to understand the years that divide
the woman of my childhood from the one here today.
My mother never believed in miracles.
She would unwittingly crush the north star
with a flap of the blinds
for fear her children would catch cold.
She believed only in her touch
the rough horizontal knowledge
of two hands swollen by lye and water.

I am thinking,
How many digressions, from childhood to today,
separate me
from this little marionette, so easily manipulated,

when she reaches her right hand beneath her seat
to touch the orange life jacket
like a child touching a book of fairytales under her bed.

Marked

My deskmate in elementary school
had blue nails, blue lips, and a big irreparable hole in his heart.
He was marked by death. He was invisible.
He used to sit on a stone
guarding our coats
as we played in the playground, that alchemy of sweat and dust.

The one marked to be king
is cold, ready for a free fall
born prematurely from a sad womb.

And the redheaded woman waiting for her drunk husband to return
will go on waiting for one hundred years.
It isn't the alcohol; she is marked by 'waiting.'
And he only as guilty as an onlooker
pushed indoors by rain.

What's more, it isn't the war
that took the life of the young boy
with melancholy eyes. He was marked as well, born to be on the recruiter's
        list.
Melancholy is the standard arsenal of war.

And then there is one marked for survival
who will continue to eat his offspring like a polar bear
that never notices the warming climate.

All of them are as closed as theorems, their sky
a rental home
where hammering even a single nail of change is forbidden.

They are waiting for their next command, which they will ignore anyway
like the Argonauts who filled their ears with wax
and rowed on through the sirens' path.

The Man Without Land

I am a man without land.
Everything I have is written diagonally across my face,
the word 'fragile' on a gift sent
during the holidays.

My grandfather grappled with his land
like a wolf in a trap
all alone in the world.

It was a fight without surprises, with intermittent ceasefires
and without flesh wounds: it was all-consuming.
His steps were enormous, his gaze like the mouth of a flesh-eating
        plant
empty and free of assumptions.

When he lost the fight
he turned around and saw
all that had happened behind him:
the manna tree grew tall, overshadowing the neighbour's yard,
his wife dead with one foot bare
and his sons aged into old bachelors.

My grandfather never built a tower. Instead, he spoke a horizontal
        language
and talked to God through it: he bought land, a lot of land. He
        bought continuity
and he swore at his creator who once told him
that he would never be able to think about tomorrow.

I am different; I am a man without land
and nothing ever happens behind my back.
I always live in the moment
like a wet piece of paper
stuck to the bumper of a truck travelling down the road.

The Madwoman's Roof

It's midnight, and a worker returning
from the second shift at the cannery
tests what strength he has left

by throwing stones against the tiles
of the madwoman's roof.

'Damn you all, you sons of bitches!'
she curses from inside.

She is history, unable to cast blame on anyone.
She is the skeleton key, the collective curse
on a night that reeks of sardines and enzymes.

The Television Owner

His roof more red than the others, and above it
the television antenna
vibrating like a shrub on the edge of a cliff –
the only one among fifty houses.

They called him 'the orphan' when he was a child
and the nickname stuck
and grew like a scar along his body.

He built his house by himself and then bought a television;
wolves attack the throat
where prey is most vulnerable.

His gate stands wide open in the evenings,
an orgy of shoes in the corridor.
'Goal!' and 'Ah!' crystallise in the air,
and his elbows tuck in during sad movies.

He never forgets a bone for his dog
and the coffee is always freshly brewed.

They call him 'the television's owner' now,
a nickname he likes. More than anyone he knows
his identity is not a question of a proper noun, but of a possessive.

He admires visitors
while they admire his blue tube.
Each envies the other. A chain.
A caravan drawn to an oasis
in the dunes.

De Jure

When his wife died
he married her sister
to buy himself some time.

Fat, childish, obsessed with cleaning
a muzzle-loading musket
she never complained. With gold earrings
and bruises he planted on her face
she had all the solemnity of a married woman.

He gave her a small plot
and she built a colony.
She gave him many children
who grew up close to the earth –
strawberries with round eyes and thorns –
shooing geese from a zone of amnesty
with gnarled sticks in their hands.

In what seemed a few minutes
his world moved from the front door
to the back stairs.

Now, exhausted, she snores with her mouth wide open
against a pillow, a supporting wall
between him and his consciousness.

Both find ways to lie to themselves:
he asking her to resist him more
and she – like the houses along the border
where the pleasure of contraband
has replaced cards on birthdays.

The Cinema

Without fail
Sundays at the cinema
were always rainy days
big black umbrellas
clashing against the ticket booth.

The doorman among the torn stubs
looked like a watercolour
hung crookedly on a kitchen wall.
We waited anxiously in the front row
looking straight ahead and
eating sunflower seeds
toasted over the ashes of textbooks
until the horizontal beam lit
a band of white dust and settled on the screen
and halos lit up over our heads –
a holy family in a Byzantine painting.

Always the same old films
soundtrack crackling like handfuls of rice
thrown at the newlyweds' white car.
Beautiful actors kissed
as if for the first time.

When the lights came on
and we saw our faces
and shook out our frozen limbs
we were an allegory for desire and disappointment
pale fences in our backyards
on which mother used to dry the laundry –
fences that were once full of colour and life.

The History Lesson

B talks about the afterlife
with the same degree of certainty
as a farmer who hangs his work clothes
behind the door late in the evening.

This is not a joke....

For years he followed the parallel lines
his paralysed father's wheelchair made,
lines, which looped into large knots
like shoelaces tied impatiently.
Years later, when his wife left him –
he recalls it was summer –
he went to the garden as usual
gathered the rotten fruit fallen at night
to avoid attracting wasps
and closed the door behind her
faintly, without anger,
the way he used to fasten the buttons
on the back of her evening dress.
The next morning, when he had breakfast, he tasted
each morsel
with gratitude
a toothless chewing
like believers seated in the front row
of church on Sunday, muttering psalms.

The children he never had
continue coming home late at night,
sweaty, filthy, and with lame excuses
on the tips of their tongues.
He listens to them
while clipping his nails, and hesitates,
a fetus preparing for birth.

History always happens somewhere else,
and like a railway keeper
clearing the sleepers of weeds and stones
or tightening a loose screw

he does not see it, but knows of power,
knows better than anyone when to get off the track
while listening with one ear against a rail.

The Smell of Milk

in memory of H. Kupi

Now
after many, many years
I can probably ask myself
how I was related to that old
cherry tree trunk of a man.

We shared plenty of time together....
When he would recount his dreams of the previous night
he moved his hands,
shovels clearing streets of snow.
He would read pages of his diary
written during the heat of the day
anticipating every comma, every word, every pause
with his forefinger,
the finger of fate, getting ahead of itself.

We would speak in English
an archaic dialect learned in prisons.
He would search out the translation
for Albanian words
trying to pronounce them with
desperate, faintly audible sounds,
grey hair stuck in a comb.

He taught me to ask 'How are you?'
while looking directly into the other's eyes.

On the mantelpiece
the photos of women in the family
alive or dead, all bent at the edges.
Their bellies, crossed by their hands
were houses nailed shut during epidemics.

It was the same every day.
Hours followed hours
until I grew impatient
or the sheep's milk would overflow into the fire.

Only later, when there were no longer diaries,
when the cherry tree was gone, when the chimney crumbled,
when the photographs faded into silence
could I smell the piercing odor of burning milk
and know that these days were coming to an end.

I was no longer a child
a child with whom the testament of reading could be trusted

...speaking to a child
is like trampling on fallen leaves
never waiting to be asked 'why' or 'how'.

A Way to Come Back

I am searching for a way to come back
something I have never been able to do before
without chipping off even a single grain from the statue of salt
a statue always facing away from me.

I will make no more promises
I will no longer believe in the pretty house
with an idyllic cloud hovering above it.
I will choose the same route, the same path I took that day I fled
following claw marks left by a bear
on tree trunks it could not climb.

I will return to pick up where history left off
like lightning
striking a furrowed field.

I will return,
simply, without time to rationalise it
like when searching for the eyes on a tight-fitting mask
or when winter approaches, smothering all fear beneath it,
a time of awakening.

NEW POEMS

Intermittent Rain

Soon
like countless woodpeckers
rain will tap at our windowpanes.

Rain will emerge from darkness
for an asteroid-moment
then plunge back again.

Silence will descend on ornate copper dishes
hung on white kitchen walls,
dishes scrubbed clean of their past.

Rain
neither sweet nor salty,
its philosophy on life neutral.
It does not stand still, does not hurry along
and it is useless to try to stop it.

From a dragon's mouth on a Viking emblem
a transparent white flame shoots forth
the eternal fire of rain.

It's Not Time For...

It's not time for a change.
For as long as I can remember
it's never been time for a change.

The house dampens. Perhaps everything is a forgery:
the wild pears, wedding rings, the milk van,
the children faltering like a tailor's pins
in an unfinished jacket
awaiting another try.

Passed from generation to generation, like haemophilia,
change is carried by the male chromosome.
You can recognise these men by their profiles –
like Caesar's face, a laurel on his head,
staring into the failure,
stamped forever on Roman coins.

Women, on the other hand,
never forget to turn on the veranda light late in the evening,
the bulb covered in mosquitoes,
believing that in spite of what they do,
what is written, will happen.

The Reason

God stiffened Pharaoh's heart: he did not let them go.
The more he resisted, the more God's power grew.
Then God left them alone again in the desert
to separate wheat from weeds among his people.

The cure for a dog's bite is Pasteur's vaccine,
nutrition imbalance – always the reason for wars.
The new technology causes floods and earthquakes.
And nadir is the reason for love.

The 'Big Wave' was Hokusai's reason for hunger.
Blindness in another painter invented the hard brush.
The reason behind all sufferings is another suffering
between generations – the silver wheel of initiation.

The reason behind Columbus's journey was not America,
nor India of gold, as he pretended.
The reason was tobacco in exchange for mirrors.
It didn't matter if he realised this or not.

Once in November, the reason and I were the same thing,
we were one. I was Rome burning, while Nero played the fiddle.
The reason why I abandon myself is not happiness.
And what comes after happiness anyway?

Now, when thinking of these, I am sitting next to a Sicilian guy
on the Alitalia flight 2389, from Rome to New York.
Perhaps there's reason here too:
his bruised palms, his one-way ticket, and his garlic breath
keep me close to the earth and far from reasons
for a while.

Two by Two

He grew up in the town beside the water,
where people answer questions with another question.

A long summer split in two,
and on the river's edges, leaves greying like sideburns.

On Sundays, four women wash clothes
slapping their men's shirts on the river rocks.
Four other women do the same thing, surrounded by foam,
taking revenge against husbands who don't exist.

Lost, by the side of the water, a confused child.
His name multiplies, his name has a shape
in the mother's palms – rounded as if a crater around her mouth
when she calls him.

The hair-clippings in the yard, on a sunny day.
A huge pair of scissors in the father's hand. No mirror.
He sits in a chair; his feet hanging down,
without touching the ground.
You are safe; the future can't find you here
the way a dog can't pick up
someone's traces in the water.

The rest of his life
he will have a duplicate view of things:
two houses, two trees to eclipse the fence, two truths,
two women to fall in love with...
Who is the reflex of whom?

He'll follow them with his Noah eyes,
as they enter and leave, two by two, like the animals do,
each time the boat strands in shallow water.

Last Journey of Rameses

Because of threatening water
they broke the statue of Rameses into blocks
and moved it to a safe and dignified place
far from where it was created.

For some hours
his Egyptian nose
hung between sky and earth
drawing the attention of a derrick-man and a part-time porter.
His sceptre hung there too, the sceptre of a man who once said:
'I carried away those whom my sword had spared
as numerous captives pinioned like birds before my horses.'

In a few days
all his broken parts will reunite
and he will be the Great Rameses again,
the star of morning and evening,
ambushed by the camera's sanguine flashes
like knives in a sailors' tavern.

But the intelligent eye
will see the geometric cuts between the blocks
not the sculpture itself but the transportation marks,
asking: 'How heavy was it?' and, 'How did they get it here?'

Like the folding lines in an over-used map
where mountains were flattened a long time ago,
roads and their conventional symbols have disappeared
and the names of cities coagulated.

Statue or statuette
the last confession doesn't belong to him, but to the shoulders of others

to that blind map circulating in pieces
which shows our only landscape
and the speed with which we traverse it.

APPENDICES

HENRY ISRAELI

Afterword: *Fresco* (2002)

In May 1996, I had the good fortune to visit Albania at a unique crossroads in its history: the five-year interlude between the fall of the Communist regime and the collapse of the governing Democratic Party. The atmosphere in Tirana was festive and full of energy. Along the main avenue in its city centre new bars and cafés, where young men and women smoked and flirted, had cropped up every few yards. There were more Mercedes-Benzes on the roads than I could count. The scene might have been lifted from a quaint Italian town but for the backdrop of Stalinist-era buildings on which were painted, in the emblematic style of Socialist Realism, workers rising against their oppressors. That, and an elderly man dragging a lamb, still very much alive, by its hind legs, its head bobbing against the pavement.

I came to Albania to meet a few poets whose voices had enthralled me, Luljeta Lleshanaku among them. Lleshanaku was the youngest by perhaps a decade, but in many ways her work felt the most experienced. The lines of her verse that fell so softly, naturally onto the page carried an immense sadness. At the same time, I was drawn to the intense yearning in her images, not a longing for an idealistic past, but for a future that could never be, as it would forever be burdened by a troublesome history. I felt myself moving through her haunting landscapes, helpless, trapped. The melancholy of these finely etched worlds seemed diametrically opposed to the new wave of optimism in downtown Tirana, yet I couldn't help feeling that the reality of Lleshanaku's poems lurked just under the city's surface.

Lleshanaku is an engaging woman with an overworked, weary, look. One sees in her, as in many Balkan people, history's raw, crushing impression. Her gaze – hungry, determined, unrelenting – is that of a survivor, someone who has overcome great adversity. We meet in her office, a large cavernous space in the institutional-looking Dajti Hotel that houses the newspaper *Zeri i rinise*, for which she serves as editor in chief. The only light in the room is from sunlight that seeps like fog through a dusty window, but in

Lleshanaku's eyes burns a birdlike energy. When she speaks, she is as direct, critical, and perversely funny as she is in her poems, where, for instance, she states that 'your breath disappearing in my lungs / is like lilies dropped into a cesspool'.

In her poetry, joy lives side by side with melancholy in a kind of symbiotic contradiction. Her lines can be exalting, playful, often bursting with a sense of wonder that is unmistakably youthful, and almost naïve. Her poems are highly imagistic, the connections between images precociously and precariously intuitive. They are, for the most part, short, contained studies, still lifes rendered abstractly, yet they soar within the boundless imagination of a speaker who delights in the sensual, the tactile, who 'light as an Indian feather... can easily reach the moon' and witnesses 'asteroids dying like drones / in ecstasy for their love, their queen'.

Her apartment building is typical for Tirana, the ground outside strewn with rubble and broken cinder blocks amongst which children and stray cats play. Inside, her apartment is small and modestly furnished. While we speak her mother serves drinks and snacks. At one point, her six-year-old daughter runs in excitedly, asking a question of Lleshanaku. The reply is given tersely, with a stern love in her voice, and the girl, satisfied, runs out again. I am comfortable here, and it's easy to forget where I am. But this is not just anywhere; this is Albania, a country where nearly every family has to some degree, at one time or another, fallen victim to oppression. Lleshanaku's family is no exception. In fact, the extent to which her family has been persecuted is sobering. Her maternal grandfather's brother fought in a pro-Allied faction against the Italian, and then German, occupiers in World War II. Directly following the war, he found himself caught in another struggle – this time on the losing side – against the Communist forces. After the Stalinists came to power, as punishment, the entire family was sentenced to five years in a prison camp. When one of Lleshanaku's uncles attempted to escape, the family was tortured. Her mother was five years old when they subjected her to electric shock. Her uncle was arrested several more times and spent a total of 27 years in prison or internment camps.

Lleshanaku's paternal grandfather, too, played an instrumental role in the anti-Communist resistance after the war, organising armed insurgencies around the country. Following his arrest, his family was also interred for many years, and he would eventually die in prison. Her mother and father obviously had much in common when they met and married in the small city of Elbasan, both families being notoriously anathema to the regime. Condemned to manual labour, her father worked as a bricklayer and her mother made woollen filters for tractors. Luljeta, born in 1968, remembers her mother arriving home each night with wounds on her hands, which she spent the evening treating so she could return to work the next morning. Together Lleshanaku's parents carried the stigma of their family's 'shame' – which Luljeta and her sister would inherit from birth.

No family member of Lleshanaku's was allowed to pursue a higher education, serve in public office, or even hold employment of any stature. They were treated as pariahs, denied any form of approval whatsoever, down to the most ludicrous detail. When a television crew arrived to film her kindergarten class singing, five-year-old Luljeta was forbidden to take part. Throughout her schooling, no matter how impressive her academic performance, her name could not appear on the honour roll. When she questioned her teachers, she was told flat out that no accolades could be accorded her because her family was not in conformity with the Communist Party. Forbidden to enter college upon graduating high school, Lleshanaku went on to hold the only kind of job the state permitted her: she worked in a carpet factory. Walking home she would pass posters and signs that were aimed directly at people like her and her family: 'Down with enemies of the working class', or 'Let us remain steadfast against our inner and foreign enemies!'

In the autumn of 1989, she married Lazer Stani – a prominent journalist for *Zeri i rinise* (ironically, the same newspaper that Lleshanaku would later head) – in a small private ceremony. A few months later, her passport was seized by the State Security and she was forbidden to leave the country, ostensibly because, according to the authorities, her cousins living in New York were collaborating against the regime. When authorities learned of her marriage, the editors of *Zeri i rinise* were given a political directive. Stani had the option of leaving his job or leaving his wife. Following his dismissal, they moved to Kllojka, a small town north of Tirana, where he was assigned a job as schoolteacher. At the same time, as petitions were being put together to return him to his job on the paper, government apparatchiks spread a rumour that Lazer and Luljeta had been killed crossing the border to Yugoslavia. But things were about to improve for the couple. The next two years would bring vast changes to Albania. In December 1990, the Communist Party accepted the presence of opposition parties, and in March 1992 free elections were held. The Democratic Party won in a landslide, promising a clean break with the past, complete freedom for its citizens, and grand investment opportunities for all.

When I met Lleshanaku in 1996, she was belatedly pursuing the college education that had earlier been denied her. In only four years she had published three noteworthy books of poetry, including *Ysmëkubizëm* (Half-Cubism), which had received much praise that year. In 1992, the poet Dritëro Agolli, who had written the introduction to her first book, *Sytë e Somnambulës* (The Sleepwalkers' Eyes), confirmed what she had always suspected – before the fall of the regime, all publishers were forbidden to publish her poetry. Of all people he should know: for 20 years he served as head of the Albanian Writers Union, the notorious arm of government censorship.

In the title-poem 'Fresco' she writes 'Freedom is meaningless', by which she means both the word and its symbols. After all, Albanians had long grown used to empty symbolism, to a society that claimed ideological superiority while simultaneously imprisoning nearly a third of its population and suppressing the basic freedoms of the rest. Real freedom, for Lleshanaku, is something bred in the imagination, something generated from the inside, not forced inward. 'In the existential ablative,' she writes in the witty poem, 'Test', 'nails sprout from my imagination / like case endings aligned / by my dead cells.' Western freedom is indicated by our ability to speak freely, openly, without fear or hesitation. To dream, to exchange ideas, to observe the human condition, the peculiarities of human relationships, to express them in verse, to have others read it...everyday choices, unnoticed by us, crucial to her.

Thirteen months after my visit, the ruling Democratic Party would be torn down in shame over an investment scandal, and the Socialist Party – including some former Communists still in prison awaiting trial for their crimes – would again be in control of the government. At the time, this was quite a blow to Lleshanaku and others who had hoped to put the Communist era behind them. Thankfully, the newly constructed Socialist Party has so far been careful about turning back the clock on personal rights, and Albania remains a free and democratic country. 'But what about Albania's future?' I recently asked Lleshanaku via e-mail. 'Like a dormant volcano,' she answered, 'throughout history the Albanian people periodically erupt – not in order to cause damage, but to prove to the world that they are still alive.' And the future of Albanian poetry? 'Albanians have no shortage of things to write about,' explained Lleshanaku, 'and they need never look far to find a rich cultural heritage. But first,' she said, 'they must search inward – not to larger cultures or overarching ideologies – to find their inner rivers.'

Luljeta Lleshanaku is young, and her poetry will surely continue to evolve. Like Albania, her work reinvents itself as outside influences continue to seep in. Her fourth collection, for example, is full of images of a New Hampshire winter where she spent two months. And yet this landscape is strangely Albanised – an isolated and lonely space that merges into the speaker's own body, a place where 'identity, weight, gravitational forces end, / where I can no longer be I'. The Albanian novelist Ridvan Dibra notes that her work is itself an attempt to open new worlds within its readers.

> When you close her book, the images don't leave you. They cleave you open like a leopard's paw, and enter into you. Once inside they create their own life, a second life, vastly different from the original. What more can we expect from real poetry, from true art?

Included in *Fresco* are poems from all four of her books, but the bulk is assembled from the mature work of her third and fourth collections. A few new poems are included here as well. They are not arranged chronologically or even thematically. Rather, the order is constructed intuitively, using the poem 'Memory,' a philosophical rumination on memory real and memory historic, as a point of departure. Although this is a book of selected poetry, it may be better referred to as a book of selected early poems. At 34 years old, Lleshanaku is extraordinarily accomplished, but there is no predicting the heights her work will climb to in years to come.

[2002]

LULJETA LLESHANAKU

Afterword: *Child of Nature* (2010)

A few years ago I was invited to spend a few months at an artists' colony in New Hampshire. While I was there I wrote several poems, but after I gained some distance from the work, I threw out almost all of them. I felt as if I was following the wrong star, as if I had falsely adapted my literary sensibilities to an American aesthetic. It was too easy to embrace the philosophy of a culture immersed in a long tradition of individualism, metaphysical perspectives, and continuity, where artists and writers simply add a stone in a wall that has been under construction for centuries. It is a philosophy completely alien to my culture.

In Albania everything happens in 24 hours. Each day you have to build a new house, a house that will probably be destroyed that same evening. Even one of our country's most famous ballads is based on the destruction of a newly built castle during the night, every night. So in Albania one must hurry to speak, even at the cost of being harsh and direct. 'Do it while you have the chance' are the words we live by. Perhaps this is the secret code of many postcolonial countries that have not been the masters of their own history, places where time means both nothing and everything. Rising from your own ashes like a phoenix and trying to enjoy the fact that you are still alive are our motivation. This basic conflict forms the background of *Child of Nature*. It is there like the faint trace of an old canvas barely visible beneath the new picture painted over it.

So what I've been doing in recent years as my life has partly shifted to America has been nothing less than reconfiguring the relationship between myself and my country, myself and my history, myself and whoever this new self is becoming. I've had to confront all the traps I had tried to escape from in the past: tradition, politics, and sentimentalism. And I think this book is mostly a reflection of this struggle.

Looking over this collection once more, I noticed that the expression 'read from the last page' is repeated (silently) in different poems, reminding me that as a child I had the odd habit of starting

149

books from the last page. I don't know how a psychologist would explain it – perhaps merely as impatience or exaggerated curiosity – but in an allegorical way it reveals how my creative process works now: I hurry to a conclusion, then go back and figure out the "why" and "how" of the poetic mechanism. At one point in the poem 'Monday in Seven Days', a child breaks apart her toys to reveal their inner mysteries. In this way I suggest that freeing objects of their function is the first step toward understanding them. One could even say that this book is simultaneously a "conclusion" and a "revelation", something that offers the tranquillity and tenderness to move closer to objects and discover what is almost impossible to see from a distance: the inner life of things.

Also important during my childhood were the characters that surrounded me. These figures were often tough men, successful at creating epics from a reality in which life was reduced to very little. And so the initial concept of this book was an album of these characters. Creating portraits in mere seconds (that is poetry's nature) was not easy. One person, my uncle Sami, never married and idealised Florence as if he had spent his honeymoon there. It was the only place he had visited outside Albania, and while he was there he got so sick from pneumonia he had to be hospitalised for several months. But to him this trip was the best thing that ever happened in his life. Uncle Sami could be cruel when he constantly shouted at us to 'Do your best!' But this was simply his way of balancing the humiliation of the Stalinist regime with an internal pride, while making sure that we were truly alive. It was difficult for a child to understand, so he repeated it systematically – we heard such words more often than we saw food on our table. The men of my family were arrogant, using this to hide their own weaknesses.

'Monday in Seven Days' is set in the small town at the foot of a mountain where I grew up. The summers are dry and small disputes arise because of the perpetual drought; weddings are crowded and unruly – revenge for our miserable lives; deaths echo long and loud through this town where nothing new ever happens. As a child I never heard the word 'paradise' or 'afterlife' mentioned when someone died, perhaps because the area was once populated by Bektashi Sufis, and according to their beliefs heaven and hell are part of this world. Or perhaps it was because a long prohibition against religious practice simplified the townspeople's concepts of life and death. Death expected nothing more than a sense of respect for the people who would miss the one departed. And then there were those men – dark, shadowy men – who sat in the empty corners of the movie theater just to hide their tears during the saddest parts of the film.

Erotic scandals were a popular topic of conversation in our town. A woman who betrayed her husband was treated much differently from the Madame Bovary we saw on television in the evening. Madame B. was contemptible, yes, but also a movie character, and therefore always an idol. Television news was also frequently discussed, and was always about another place, never fresh, purified by distance, and skimmed over with apathy. Sunday shopping at the peasants' market (the only private market permitted by the government) and the men returning home with fresh green vegetables or an occasional piece of handmade cheese or butter, was always an interesting event, one that had less to do with hunger than with the fact that they had bought something actually produced in one's private garden or home, rather than in a factory or a cooperative.

The calm setting I am describing was interrupted most often by two people: Mustafa, the town drunk, and Zyhra, an abandoned woman. Mustafa was a good target for everybody, a person to make fun of, a tortoise at a funeral or, as I say in one of my poems, a 'swab of alcohol-dabbed cotton / pressed to a wound'. Zyhra always dressed in rags, rarely stepped out of her house, and was thus a mysterious and intriguing character, especially to children as, in general, the only other mysterious thing we ever saw was a nightmare – the "jeep" that was the secret service car coming to make arrests.

There were also the Friday gypsies, women who pretended to read fortunes in threads cut from our clothes in exchange for a piece of bread or cheese, or some oil. Everybody knew they were fakes, but Friday night's sleep was different – magical and hopeful because of their predictions. I also can't forget my neighbour, the madwoman, the one who used to wander the streets and talk in a loud voice to the ghosts of executed ministers or dead politicians. Politics, even in her darkness, was with her everywhere!

There were only a few books on our shelves – the people of our town regarded books with suspicion. The most educated generation of Albanians belonged to the 19th century and the beginning of the 20th, when we were still part of the Ottoman Empire. But when I grew up it was different. It was an era of forbidden books, books that were victims of the cultural revolution, mostly translated Russian classics: Turgenev, Tolstoy, Chekhov, and sometimes an American like Walt Whitman. I never understood why these books were banned, but because of the public library's 'circulation conspiracy' – books suddenly disappearing from the shelves – we were obsessed with these titles. When a friend of mine discovered Camus's writings were sequestered in the library's R-sector of blacklisted books, he used all of his connections to see them. But the moment Camus was no longer forbidden, he lost interest in his work.

The end of the Communist regime was followed by a period of rationalisation, when people started to question the meanings behind everything. But it seems as if it is even more difficult for Albanians to write now than ever before, the same way learning to swim is much easier as a child when one has a narrower sense of danger, than when one is an adult and fear becomes greater than the desire to swim. Now, exposed to the wide range of world literature, Albanian writers are suddenly conscious that the water we've been swimming in is much deeper than we had thought.

In the end I think I returned to my initial motivation for writing in *Child of Nature*: simply to record some of the things I saw, heard, and felt, letting the voices of three generations of Albanians who may have thought with loud voices but couldn't speak, filter through. As the saying goes, reveal certain facts and *res ipsa loquitur*, the thing speaks for itself.

[2010]

Acknowledgements

FRESCO

I would like to thank Joanna Goodman for sweating over some of the translations and helping to edit and arrange the rest, Caroline Crumpacker for her advice on ordering the poems, Peter Constantine for introducing the selection in more ways than one, and Peter Glassgold, Peggy Fox, Barbara Epler, Declan Spring, and all the staff of New Directions who made this book possible.

I would also like to extend my gratitude for the hard work and long hours contributed by all the Albanian translators; in particular Ukzenel Bucpapa and Shpresa Qatipi, who shouldered the brunt of the work. Without their invaluable participation this collection would not have been possible. I also owe Dr Bucpapa very sincere thanks for first introducing me to the work of Luljeta Lleshanaku. I am indebted as well to Albana Lleshanaku for enduring many hours of questions regarding the particularities of interpreting translations from the Albanian.

[HI]

CHILD OF NATURE

Some of these poems first appeared in the anthology *Between Water and Song: New Poets for the Twenty-first Century* (White Pine Press), and in the following journals: *American Poetry Review, Cerise, Lana Turner, Many Mountains Moving, Per Contra, Pleiades, Quiddity, Southern Humanities Review, Washington Square, Witness* and *Words Without Borders.*

I would like to thank the Black Mountain Institute at the University of Nevada, Las Vegas, for a very generous fellowship that allowed me to work on this book.

For my niece and nephew, Vesa and Gemi Miftari, to whom I offer this in place of distance.

[LL]

Bibliography

POEMS LISTED BY BOOKS

The Sleepwalker's Eyes (Sytë e Somnambulës, Artemida, 1992): 'And the Sun Us Extinguished'; 'Our Words Have Grown Old.'

Sunday Bells (Këmbanat e Së Dielës, Shtëpia Botuese e Lidhjes së Shkrimatarëve, 1994): 'Perhaps My Mother'; 'The Night Will Soon Be Over...'; 'Sunday Bells'; 'Absence'; 'Silence'; 'The Habitual'; 'The Moon in November'; 'The Almshouse'; 'Self-Defence'; 'Night Landscape.'

Half-Cubism (Ysmëkubizëm, Eurorilindja, 1996): 'Peninsula'; 'Neurosis'; 'Winter'; 'Nocturne. Soft Whistle'; 'More Than a Retrospective'; 'What Is Known'; 'Fresco'; 'Electrolytes'; 'Test'; 'So Long As'; 'The Bed'; 'Frail Bones'; 'Once Again About My Father'; 'Yearly Snow'; 'Chronic Appendicitis'; 'The Awakening of the Eremite'; 'Out of Boredom'; 'Quite by Accident'; 'No Time'; 'Farewell, Sunny Days'; 'Half-Cubism'; 'Seasons Change.'

Antipastoral (Antipastorale, Eurorilindja, 1999): 'Memory'; 'The Woman and the Scissors'; 'The Woman and the Giraffes'; 'Chamomile Breath'; 'Clear Hours'; 'Always a Premonition'; 'With a Piercing Clarity'; 'Over the icy magma of your gray curiosity'; 'Frost'; 'Truth'; 'Within Another Idiom'; 'Betrayed'; 'Only the Beginning'; 'Half Past Three'; 'On a Night Like This'; 'Antipastoral'; 'Heathen Rejoicing'; 'In the Home of the Dead Man'; 'Watching Them Nap'; 'A Mutual Understanding.'

New Poems: 'Birds and Carbon'; 'The Blossoming Almond Branch'; 'Still Life.'

Index of titles and first lines

(Titles are shown in italics, first lines in roman type.)

155

159